Essential Histories

# War in Japan 1467–1615

## Essential Histories

# War in Japan 1467–1615

Stephen Turnbull

First published in Great Britain in 2002 by Osprey Publishing,
Midland House, West Way, Botley, Oxford OX2 0PH, UK
44-02 23rd St, Suite 219, Long Island City, NY 11101, USA
E-mail: info@ospreypublishing.com

Transferred to digital print on demand 2009

First published 2002
4th impression 2008

Printed and bound by Cadmus Communications, USA

A CIP catalogue record for this book is available from the British Library

ISBN: 978 1 84176 480 1

Editorial by Thomas Lowres
Design by Ken Vail Graphic Design, Cambridge, UK
Cartography by The Map Studio
Index by Alison Worthington
Picture research by Image Select International
Origination by PPS Grasmere, Leeds, UK
Typeset in Monotype Gill Sans and ITC Stone Serif

**Dedication**
To my brother-in-law on the occasion of his sixtieth birthday.

**Author's Note and Acknowledgements**
In keeping with the spirit of the Essential Histories series, I have tried to produce a concise and readable account of Japan's most
turbulent age. This has been an enormous task because the wars of the time were complex affairs, complicated by shifting patterns of
alliance and rapid developments in weaponry and tactics. I include all these factors in the pages which follow, and describe every
major battle of the period in some way. Those chosen for detailed study, however, do not include battes such as Nagashino which are
already covered in other Osprey volumes.
I would like to thank the Royal Armouries for their cooperation and also the many institutions and museums in Japan. As usual my wife
provided all the administrative back-up.

FOR A CATALOGUE OF ALL BOOKS PUBLISHED BY OSPREY
MILITARY AND AVIATION PLEASE CONTACT:

Osprey Direct, c/o Random House Distribution Center,
400 Hahn Road, Westminster, MD 21157
Email: uscustomerservice@ospreypublishing.com

Osprey Direct, The Book Service Ltd, Distribution Centre,
Colchester Road, Frating Green, Colchester, Essex, CO7 7DW
E-mail: customerservice@ospreypublishing.com

**www.ospreypublishing.com**

# Contents

# Introduction

In Kyoto, Japan's ancient capital, there is a temple of gold and a temple of silver. Both have tragic tales to tell. They are separated from each other in time by a century, in space by the entire breadth of the city, and in their history by the great division in human experience between peace and war.

The temple of gold was built in 1394 by Ashikaga Yoshimitsu, the third shogun of the Ashikaga dynasty, as a symbol of peace. Under his rule the bitter divisions between rival emperors had been repaired, as had the wars on their behalf that had scarred the face of the 14th century. Japan was also reconciled with the new Ming dynasty of China, having laid to rest the fear and mistrust that had arisen from the terrible Mongol invasions. Trade with China was now restored, and into Japan flowed silks and spices, while out of it went consignments of that most deadly of export items, the Japanese sword. As peace broke out all around him, a satisfied Yoshimitsu retired to his new mansion in Kitayama on the north-western hills of Kyoto, where the Kinkakuji, a building covered from floor to roof in gold leaf, was reflected in a lake of lotus blossoms and shone like the golden sun.

Almost a hundred years passed. Yoshimitsu's grandson Yoshimasa was now shogun. He had no particular peacemaking initiatives to boast about, but then there had been a century of calm prior to his accession, broken only by the odd rebellion which the shugo, the shogun's loyal deputies who governed the provinces, always seemed to quell with ease. Even the Japanese pirates had been vanquished: a few exemplary beheadings had worked wonders.

Then, in 1467, a war called the Onin War broke out in Kyoto itself, and seemed so unending that in 1474 Ashikaga Yoshimasa decided to withdraw from the horrors

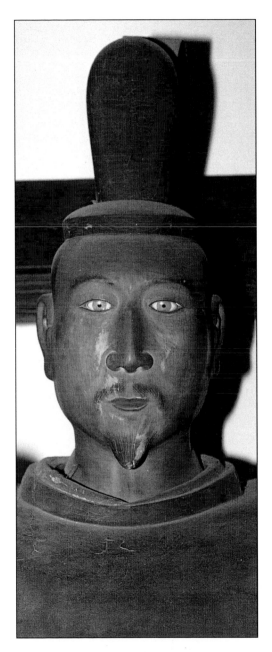

The shogun Ashikaga Yoshimasa, whose neglect of government was partly responsible for the outbreak of the Onin War, which plunged Japan into the chaos of the Sengoku Period.

around him. Emulating his illustrious grandfather, Yoshimasa built his own temple – of silver – at Higashiyama, on the eastern hills. The Ginkakuji was still incomplete when Yoshimasa died in 1490; most noticeably of all, it lacked the covering of silver that had given the temple its name. The silver never came, and if one visits the Ginkakuji today all that is to be seen is an exquisite little wooden pavilion that almost blends in with the surrounding trees. Where the Kinkakuji is brilliant, the Ginkakuji is sombre; where the Kinkakuji shines in the midday sun, the Ginkakuji fades into the shadows of the evening. It is at its best by moonlight, because the builders left a pile of white sand in the courtyard, and poetic fancy saw in it the shape of Mount Fuji. So the gardeners went out with bamboo rakes and created Japan's first Zen garden.

As thousands of visitors have discovered over the centuries, Kinkakuji is for looking at, while Ginkakuji is for looking from, and so Ashikaga Yoshimasa could sit and gaze across the white sea of raked sand to the sculpted pine trees beyond the lake. From inside the building he would, mercifully, be spared not only the sight of the bare wooden timbers that mocked him with their absence of silver, but also the other consequence of the financial extravagance, mismanagement and neglect that had caused the diminution of his pet project and seriously weakened the shogunate itself. He could not see it, but he may well have heard it above the birdsong, the hum of the cicadas and the croaking of frogs. There, in the background, was the unmistakable sound of war. While Yoshimasa contemplated his peaceful garden, the capital city in which it lay was being burned to the ground.

## Sengoku: the age of war

The Onin War, the conflict that had so depressed Yoshimasa, ushered in a time of such unparalleled strife that future historians, puzzling over what to call a century and a half of war in Japan, threw up their hands in despair and settled for an analogy with the most warlike period in ancient Chinese history: the Age of Warring States. Translated into Japanese this became the Sengoku jidai or Sengoku Period, and the name stuck. It was an age when rival warlords, called *daimyo* (literally 'the great names') fought one another with armies of samurai – for land, for survival and, in some cases, even for that seemingly most empty of prizes, the control of the shogun himself and his devastated capital.

It is impossible to understand the wars of the Sengoku Period merely by looking at

their chronological sequence. Instead it is more profitable to approach the conflict in terms of two overlapping processes: fission and fusion. The process of fission was sparked by the Onin War and resulted in numerous little wars taking place all over Japan. As these happened in areas geographically remote from one another, they have to be regarded as separate manifestations of a similar process; it is also important to note that these similar events, in different parts of Japan, could be separated by several decades. During the year 1584, for example, two rival

The Ginkakuji, or silver pavilion, built by Ashikaga Yoshimasa, and the most poignant memorial of his reign. We are looking across the white sand garden to the little wooden building that was never covered in silver as had been intended.

*daimyo* on Japan's southern island of Kyushu were still fighting their wars of fission, while at Komaki in central Japan a different war was taking place that properly belongs in the succeeding process of fusion.

The two rivals in the Komaki campaign were the second and third of three

## The provinces of Japan during the Sengoku Period

Japan was historically divided into these provinces until they were replaced by the modern prefectures late in the 19th century. During the Sengoku Period Kyoto was the capital, but was supplanted in influence by the establishment of the Tokugawa shogunate in Edo (now Tokyo) in 1603.

'super-*daimyo*' who were eventually to restore Japan to united rule under one sword. Within three years of Komaki, the second of this trio, Toyotomi Hideyoshi, was to cross over into Kyushu and impose his own fusion on the local fission. Finally, in 1603, the third unifier, Tokugawa Ieyasu, just happened to have the right pedigree from the ancient Minamoto family to allow him to revive the shogunate. With the final defeat of his rivals at Osaka in 1615, the Tokugawa shoguns took over where the Ashikaga had left off, and the Age of Warring States gave way to the long Tokugawa Peace, out of which, two and a half centuries later, was born modern Japan.

# Chronology

# Loyalty to the shogun collapses

The men who did the fighting during the Sengoku Period were the samurai ('those who serve'), Japan's equivalent of the European knight. Before the Onin War began, these men already had a glorious military history that spanned several generations. They entered Japanese history as elite mounted archers. In ancient times horses had been known only as beasts of burden, and the Japanese first saw them used in war during one of their early expeditions in Korea. In the first five centuries of the Christian era Korea was ruled by the three rival kingdoms of Koguryo, Silla and Paekche. Kinship ties with Paekche meant that Japan inevitably became involved in the conflict and in about AD400 a Japanese army, sent to support Paekche and composed entirely of foot soldiers, was heavily defeated in battle by a Koguryo army riding horses. Within a century of this event there is archaeological evidence of horses being ridden in Japan.

The plains of eastern Japan proved ideal for horse breeding and pasturing, and as riding skills developed, so did the notion of cavalry warfare, with mounted archery becoming the preferred technique. In 553 Paekche once again sought Japanese help, and this time asked specifically for 'a large supply of bows and horses', thus indicating that the combination of horsemanship and archery was now firmly established in Japan.

The rise of the samurai as an elite military aristocracy developed slowly during the following centuries, and it was mounted archery that became their hallmark in the wars of the 10th–12th centuries. Many hours were given to practising the skills of loosing a bow at full gallop, a technique that survives today as the martial art of yabusame. By contrast, the lowly foot soldiers carried *naginata* (glaives), and always acted in a secondary role. As a result of the Gempei War of 1180–85 one samurai clan, the Minamoto, triumphed over its rivals, the Taira, to set up a military dictatorship under the first shogun. The triumph of the mounted samurai archer was now complete and remained unassailable until the battles against the Mongol invasions of 1274 and 1281. These wars provided an unusual challenge because their Mongol opponents fought in strange ways, such as delivering random volleys of arrows, but once the 1281 invasion had been disposed of by the famous typhoon called the kamikaze, the samurai could return to the mode of warfare they understood.

Although much of the fighting of the 14th-century civil wars involved the defence of castles in wooded mountains, there was still the occasional open battle such as Minatogawa (1336) and Shijo-Nawate (1348), where mounted samurai were used, and these demonstrate that there had been little change in cavalry tactics from the 12th century. When samurai took on samurai, there was no need to fight in any other way, and horsemen could still easily overcome infantry out in the open. One account notes acutely how 'foot soldiers may be strong, but they are not strong enough to stop arrows; they may be fast, but not fast enough to outrun horses'.

The mounted archers naturally preferred to operate on open ground, and one reason for the frequent references to arson in the chronicles is their need to create such an open space artificially. The greatest danger from anyone on foot came from a samurai with a bow, who might climb on to the roofs of buildings and pick off individual horsemen; only in situations like that could dismounted troops hope to triumph over the samurai on horseback.

Yet at this point in history came the creation of the greatest challenge so far to traditional samurai cavalry tactics, when generals realised that one way to use the numerous foot soldiers in their armies was to take away their edged weapons and give them bows. They could pour volleys of arrows into an enemy, much as the Mongol archers had done. This was the complete antithesis of the notion of the elite mounted archer delivering one arrow with great precision, and the mounted enemy did, of course, provide an excellent target for this new technique. A samurai who responded merely by galloping forward and loosing a few arrows into a mass of foot archers was unlikely to discourage the foot soldiers, who would reply with scores of arrows of their own. This is precisely what happened when samurai horsemen of the Hosokawa were trapped on the edge of Lake Biwa and came under fire from men in boats:

*They could not pass to the north because they had not finished burning the dwellings of Otsu. A deep lake to the east was likewise impassable, forcing the Hosokawa army to advance in single file along a narrow road. The enemy rowed parallel to the Hosokawa and shot them from the side, killing five hundred in all.*

It was armies such as these that often came to blows in the early decades of the 15th century, but their conflicts were always local affairs, and there was still a universal respect for the institution of the shogun, even if the current incumbent spent all his time performing the tea ceremony and neglecting his role as 'military dictator'. Indeed, so peaceful were the times that the shugo may have fought one another on occasion, but they were sufficiently confident of peace that they maintained mansions within Kyoto, where the calm was greatest of all.

It was therefore doubly tragic that the protagonists in the Onin War, the Yamana and the Hosokawa, should own mansions close enough together for rivalry to be openly expressed by fighting, and far enough away to allow a no-man's land between them once that rivalry had exploded into arson and archery attacks. Others joined in, and, fearful of being caught in vulnerable Kyoto, they took the cause of either Yamana or Hosokawa out to the provinces, where it was quickly realised that the undying respect for the shogun had been one of the Onin War's first casualties. Province by province and year by year the process of fission continued, until almost all of Japan was engulfed in the opportunistic wars of the Sengoku Period.

Because of their isolation on the edges of Kyoto, both the gold and the silver temples survived the 10-year-long Onin War. Most of the centre of the ancient capital was reduced to a charred wasteland, and it soon became apparent that the conflict that had begun in that fateful year of Onin was going to be no ordinary war. That Kyoto itself had been involved at all was uniquely sad, but the most worrying feature of all was how the fighting had spread. Local landowners remote from the capital, all of whom had once pledged loyalty to the shogun, had almost been forced into taking sides with one of the two families whose initial differences of opinion had already brought tragedy to Kyoto. Some of the provincial shugo tried loyally and vainly to assert the shogun's authority, but they were pushed aside. Others quietly threw off their allegiance to that increasingly questionable institution, while a few shugo were even murdered and had their places taken by opportunists who recognised the true trend of the times. Others simply reinvented themselves. No longer was a shugo merely the shogun's 'deputy for such-and-such province'; he was now, simply, the province's *daimyo* – its ruler.

As the Sengoku Period got under way Japan saw the disappearance from history of names that had gone back centuries to some illustrious ancestor and their replacement by warlords whose only claim to fame was their own, not their forebears', success in war. Among them were some who had managed to retain their ancestral holdings, and some who had stolen land from the defeated. They included ex-aristocrats, ex-foot soldiers,

The *daimyo* (great names) were the warlords who took advantage of the weakness of the shogunate to establish their own petty kingdoms. In this exhibit in Kokura castle we see a *daimyo* consulting with his senior retainers.

ex-pirates, ex-farmers and at least one ex-oil merchant. Together they made the Sengoku Period: the great age of war in Japan. This was the most violent, turbulent, cruel and exciting time in Japanese history – a period that began with wars fought with bow and arrow from wooden stockades and ended with stone castles bombarded with cannon. It was an age that began with an isolated Japan where the wars of continental East Asia had little influence, and ended with a Japan that traded with Europe and sent mercenaries to fight abroad. It began with a country fearful of the memory of foreign invasion and ended with a country dissolved into its own civil war, exhausted from a disastrous foreign invasion of its own.

# Rival samurai armies

During the Sengoku Period the nature of the armies of the warring sides was remarkably similar whichever pair or group of *daimyo* were fighting, so that any differences in army composition or tactics depended much more on the *daimyo*'s resources and on the evolution of samurai warfare over the century and a half than any personal preferences. It is therefore more profitable to examine the make-up of the typical samurai army of the Sengoku Period.

Although the structure of a *daimyo*'s army changed greatly over time, there was always a basic distinction between the samurai and the foot soldier. At the time of the Onin War the samurai were still the elite troops, the officer corps, the aristocracy, while the foot soldiers were lower class warriors recruited from the *daimyo*'s estate workers. Over the years the lawlessness of the times led to another source of supply for foot soldiers, and a *daimyo*'s loyal and long-standing infantry found themselves fighting beside – and often outnumbered by – men casually recruited into an army, enticed by the prospect of loot. These men were called ashigaru (light feet). They could fight well when the occasion demanded, but they were also notorious for deserting. The successful *daimyo* were the ones who recognised that ashigaru needed discipline and training to produce modern infantry squads, and soon the term ashigaru began to be applied to any non-samurai soldier who fought on foot.

All ranks of a samurai army were well protected in the typical suit of iron and leather armour, made from small scales of metal, lacquered for rust prevention and then laced together. When guns were introduced, breastplates were made out of solid iron plates. A samurai's helmet would be a substantial affair of lacquered iron, while the ashigaru wore simpler conical iron hats.

The samurai would be armed with a bow or a spear, with the latter predominating. The bow was a longbow, shot from one-third of the way up its length, but the most famous weapon of the samurai was of course his sword. These two-handed weapons were masterpieces of metalwork, with resilient springy bodies and razor-sharp cutting edges. Their legendary blades were of multiple construction, hammered many times to produce the required strength and flexibility

A typical suit of armour for a samurai of the Sengoku Period. It is made of small plates of lacquered iron fastened together.

to allow the weapon to be used as both sword and shield. A dagger with an equally sharp blade would also be worn. Foot soldiers were armed with either arquebuses, spears or bows, and all also carried a sword. Some carried flags, drums or the samurai's personal equipment.

## The samurai spearman

One of the most important developments in samurai warfare during the Sengoku Period was the emergence of large-scale infantry tactics, in an exact parallel to what was happening in 16th-century Europe. However, although infantry warfare became increasingly common, it never completely replaced cavalry warfare, largely because generals found a combination of both to be to their best advantage.

There was another, more subtle, factor at work too, because throughout Japanese history generals had cherished the notion that samurai were innately superior to foot soldiers, and samurai had traditionally been seen primarily as mounted men. Indeed, the popular notion of 'the samurai swordsman', so beloved of the movie industry, owes more to the time when wars had ceased than to actual battlefield experience, when the cherished image was not of a soldier who wielded a sword on foot, but of a man who rode a horse. The major change that occurred in the context of horseback fighting was therefore not its overall decline, but a radical change in how mounted warfare was carried out. This was the remarkable development, so often glossed over in historical accounts, which saw the mounted samurai archer of the earlier centuries transformed into the mounted samurai spearman, as the battle for superiority between cavalry and infantry swung from one side to the other.

The stimulus for this development – the most important change in cavalry tactics in the whole of samurai history – was the practice noted earlier of using foot solders as missile troops, along with the growing trend

towards large armies. Somehow the samurai horseman had to hit back at these missile troops, and he needed to use his mobility and striking power to provide the shock of a charge against the ashigaru. The problem was that a samurai carried a bow, which was an encumbrance in hand-to-hand fighting, and even if the bow was given to an attendant, swords were of limited use from the saddle. In a dramatic change to established practice, the bow was abandoned in favour of the spear, and the mounted archer gave way to the mounted spearman. Some mounted archers were retained, operating as mobile sharpshooters, but the majority of samurai now carried spears fitted with blades that were every bit as sharp as their swords. Some samurai preferred short spear blades, while others liked long ones. Some spears were fitted with crossblades to pull an opponent from his saddle, and all would be protected from the weather when not in use by a lacquered wooden scabbard. Yabusame (mounted archery) was replaced by spear techniques from the saddle, and for the first time in Japanese history a samurai army could deliver something recognisable as a cavalry charge.

Takeda Shingen was the greatest exponent of the new style of mounted fighting, whether it was against archers or ashigaru firing the arquebuses that began to replace bows from about 1560. At Uedahara in 1548 and Mikata ga Hara in 1572 the Takeda cavalry rode down disorganised infantry missile units. At Uedahara the ashigaru had a few primitive Chinese handguns, but at Mikata ga Hara it was the arquebus that was defeated, as described later in this book.

For a few decades, at least, the initiative had shifted back in favour of the mounted man, yet armies were probably never exclusively mounted. Even though the most common expression for the Takeda is *kiba gundan* (mounted 'war band' or 'army'), in reality this was not composed exclusively of horsemen. Instead the typical Sengoku war band was a mixture of cavalry and infantry. At Mikata ga Hara, Ieyasu's samurai could not withstand what was described in all the

An early development during the Sengoku Period involved the mounted samurai archer exchanging his bow for a spear, thus enabling him to deliver a cavalry charge. This display at the Ise Sengoku Village represents the charge of the Takeda at Nagashino in 1575.

chronicles as a cavalry charge, even though many of the so-called 'cavalry' were on foot. If horsemen charged the enemy on their own they could deliver a reasonable impact, but in reality, for a complete breakthrough on the battlefield, they went into the attack on foot alongside the ashigaru.

It is also important to note that the horses of those days were different from those we see in samurai films. The Sengoku horses were much smaller, as was confirmed in 1989 when archaeologists dug up a horse's skeleton at Tsutsuji ga saki, the Takeda capital. Its height to the shoulder was 120cm, and its weight was estimated as 250kg, which compares to 160cm and 500kg for a modern thoroughbred, so the shock of a charge hitting the enemy ranks would have been much less. The speed of a modern thoroughbred would also be greater, and as the Sengoku horse had to bear an armoured horseman, its pace would be further reduced. As noted above, they were usually accompanied by soldiers and attendants on foot, running as fast as they could, and who

could not be left behind, so a Sengoku cavalry charge cannot have been as severe as it is popularly depicted.

The well-organised Takeda cavalry habitually used a tactical scheme which involved dividing their enemy, luring them on and then swiftly attacking. For this to succeed, the classic notion of heroic one-to-one combat could no longer be the central feature of a battle. Instead group operations became the norm, where the mutually supportive band of mounted samurai and ashigaru charged furiously against the enemy men and horses. This is the background to the reputation of the Takeda army that had them feared as *shinshu oniyaku* (holy devils) because of their numerous superior horses, adapted to mountainous terrain and carrying well-trained riders.

# The infantry response

The many battles of the Sengoku Period therefore became a contest between the shock of a cavalry charge and the firepower of infantry. At first the replacement of the samurai's bow with the spear meant that horsemen began to dominate the battlefield again, but after the Takeda cavalry victories of Ueda and Mikata ga Hara, the balance began to shift back in favour of the infantry. The main reason for this was the introduction of the arquebus, a simple musket fired by dropping a lighted match on to a pan when you pulled the trigger. The arquebus had been the standard European infantry missile weapon for many years, having proved its worth at battles such as Cerignola in Italy, 1503, and their introduction to Japan is commonly dated to the year 1543 when a shipwreck deposited a group of Portuguese traders and their arquebuses on to the shores of the island of Tanegashima. The Shimazu *daimyo*, who owned Tanegashima, is recorded as using arquebuses of his own manufacture, copied from the original specimens, in battle in 1549, but the two main proponents of arquebus use, and the leaders in the development of infantry firearms tactics, were Japan's two deadliest enemies – the 'super-*daimyo*' Oda Nobunaga and the religious fanatics of the Ikko-ikki.

Nobunaga's father had been an early firearms enthusiast, and in 1550 the young Nobunaga had stunned his future father-in-law, Saito Dosan, by parading in front of him with 500 arquebuses. In the case of the Ikko-ikki, these lower-class warriors appreciated better and sooner than most *daimyo* that, in spite of its slow loading time and its inaccuracy, a simple peasant could be trained to use an arquebus in a fraction of the time it took to develop the skills and the strong arm muscles of an expert archer. The arquebus also had a greater penetrating power over a longer range; all that was needed was to have enough of them, a problem the Ikko-ikki solved by developing their own gun

foundries. However, both the Ikko-ikki and Oda Nobunaga also came to the conclusion that although effective firepower was vital for shifting the balance back from cavalry to infantry again, it was still not quite the whole story. As late as Mikata ga Hara in 1572, the Takeda horsemen were to be found riding down disorganised arquebusiers who had fired their weapons and were then caught reloading.

There were two answers to this problem: to train the arquebusiers to fire in controlled repeating volleys and to give them some form of reassurance, if not an absolute guarantee, that they could give their full attention to reloading without having to worry about defending themselves against approaching horsemen. Volley firing appears to have been used for the first time by Oda Nobunaga in 1554 at Muraki castle, but this was done by relays of men firing across a castle moat, and Nobunaga himself seems to have been surprised in his turn when the Ikko-ikki of Nagashima used similar techniques against him in a field battle in 1573. As for the extra protection while reloading, the simplest solution was to create squads of ashigaru spearmen whose role was to provide a hedge of spears for their comrades, rather like European pikemen. Field defences could also be built, and a smaller number of skilled archers could fill any gaps in the arquebusiers' rhythm by loosing volleys of their own.

Both solutions are illustrated by one of the most famous battles of the Sengoku Period. At Nagashino in 1575 Oda Nobunaga lined up 3,000 arquebusiers, protected by spearmen and a rough wooden palisade, and the illustrious mounted samurai of the Takeda were almost broken by the gunfire. It is important to remember, however, that many hours of fierce hand-to-hand fighting followed before the battle was over: it was the shock of the charge that was broken, not

*The most effective response to a cavalry charge was from massed ranks of infantry firing volleys of arquebus bullets. Here, reproduction arquebuses are fired at the annual festival to commemorate the battle of Nagashino.*

every member of the Takeda cavalry. It is also interesting that Oda Nobunaga's use of three ranks of rapid volley firing at Nagashino does not seem to have been repeated. This may be because the concentration needed by his gunners was facilitated by the defence works. In most subsequent cases two ranks of arquebus fire seems to have been the maximum possible, and several contemporary illustrations show a smaller number of archers standing beside the arquebusiers, while the spearmen stand ready to form a defensive hedge. Unlike field fortifications, which did not suit the fluid nature of most samurai warfare and make only rare appearances such as at Okita Nawate in 1584, the ashigaru spearmen squads became a regular feature. They were trained by their *daimyo* to receive cavalry by making a *yari fusuma* ('ring of steel'; literally a blanket of spears). As one chronicler put it:

*If a person on foot has a sword as the personal weapon and the horseman a spear, above everything else kill the horse, but it is even good to cut through the bridle. Again, if when on foot the spear is one's weapon it is good to thrust inside the opponent's helmet or into the armpit.*

As Nagashino demonstrated so well, the effects of the initial disciplined arquebus fire could make a tremendous difference to the outcome of a battle. In some cases, such as in the Battle of Tennoji in 1615, with which the siege of Osaka concluded, troops were forced into precipitate action by arquebus fire.

The mounted spearman may have represented an ideal of samurai behaviour, but on many occasions during the Sengoku Period samurai chose to dismount and fight on foot in infantry formations. Few samurai were now too proud to risk the outcome of a battle for their own glory, yet whatever sophisticated battlefield tactics existed at this late stage in samurai history, the greatest achievement remained unchanged since the time of the Gempei Wars: to be the first into battle and to take the head of a worthy opponent. As a result, for every description in the chronicles of a samurai general

A willingness to perform the act of *seppuku* or *hara kiri* was one of the defining marks of the samurai. In this print by Yoshitoshi, a warrior prepares to kill himself using his *tanto* (dagger).

painstakingly arranging his arquebus squads, there are a dozen telling of individual combat in a way that would not have disgraced the hyperbole of the *Heike Monogatari*, the great chronicle of the 12th century. Cavalry tactics were therefore always prized, but realism determined that they could never exist independently of infantry warfare. There also had to be the combination of arms, with full cooperation between units, if a battle was to be won.

## Japanese castles and siegework

During the Sengoku Period, just as many battles took place in a siege situation as on an open battlefield, and this led to the development of a particular style of castle design and type of siege warfare, reflected today in the beautiful castle keeps that have survived. When the Sengoku Period began, castles were fairly rudimentary structures known as *yamashiro* (mountain castles), which refers to the fact that these fortresses were not merely built on mountains, but built almost literally *from* mountains. The forest cover was stripped away and the gaps between adjacent ridges were excavated to make ditches. By carving up the mountain in such a way a roughly concentric series of mountain peaks could be converted into a number of natural inner and outer baileys to create interlocking fields of fire. Ditches were strengthened by having vertical cross pieces through them built at right angles to the inner walls. Near perpendicular sections were made more dramatic by having long channels cut out of them, down which rocks could be rolled. Mountain streams were diverted into gullies to create moats, and entrances to gateways were offset to allow an enemy's approach to be covered completely.

At the same time more elaborate walls and buildings were raised and substantial

A fibreglass samurai mans the wall of a castle at the Ise Sengoku Village.

surrounding walls built using a form of wattle and daub construction, with arrow ports cut at regular intervals. To keep weather damage to a minimum the walls were topped with sloping thatch, wooden shingles or even tiles. In many cases the walls were supported on their insides by a series of horizontal and vertical timbers, and at times of attack planks were laid across these to provide platforms from which guns or bows could be fired over the walls. Similar platforms could also be fitted to gates.

The great weakness of the *yamashiro* was the inherent instability of the natural foundations where the forest cover had been removed. Three storeys was the absolute maximum that could be risked for an enclosed tower with rooms, and outlook towers tended to be mere skeletal structures. To bind the soil on exposed sections, the grass was allowed to grow, but the torrential rain experienced in Japan took a heavy toll of foundations and structures alike. If stronger, and therefore heavier, structures such as keeps and gatehouses were to be added, then something more substantial than a grassy bank was needed as a castle base, and the solution to this problem would provide Japanese castles with their most enduring visual features. These were the great stone bases, a fundamental design

element which can be identified at even the most ruined castle site. In essence, the stone bases were created by cladding the excavated hillsides first with two layers of hammered pebbles and then with a final layer of massive, partly dressed stones without mortar. The new style of stone castle did not immediately supplant the earlier models, however: even as late as the 1590s examples drawn from the entire history of castle development were still in use.

The moat and walls of Hikone castle, a good example of the Japanese style of castle building.

The introduction of stone as a building material not only solved the problem of soil erosion and weather damage, but it also allowed castle designers to raise structures that would previously have been impossible, leading to the Japanese castle as we know it today. Stone castle bases sloped outwards dramatically, both to hold back the inner

Inuyama castle, which is built on top of a wooded
mountain next to the Kiso river. This detail shows the use
of stone, wood and plaster daub as construction materials.

core (which in the case of a stone castle on a
flat surface, such as much of Osaka castle,
had to be artificially created) and to take the
weight of a keep. There was also the far from
trivial threat of earthquakes, which occur
frequently in Japan. It was found that long
and gently sloping stone walls absorbed
earthquake shocks very well.

The first tower keeps were less ornate
structures than those commonly seen today,
but when embellished to the extent revealed
by many extant specimens, the keep made a
dramatic statement of a *daimyo*'s power.
Unlike almost anywhere else in the typical
Japanese castle, the windows, roofs and
gables of the keep are arranged in the most
subtle, harmonious and intricate patterns.
However, they were always primarily
fortresses, and they witnessed some of the
fiercest fighting of the Sengoku Period.

## Strategic communications

There was more to achieving victory on a
Sengoku battlefield than sending one's
samurai spearmen forward in an impetuous
charge against a line of foot soldiers or a
castle wall. Good logistics were needed, and
these were underpinned by robust
communications systems within a *daimyo*'s
province, and equally efficient ones on the
micro level of the battlefield.

The most important strategic
communications function was that of rapidly
transmitting throughout one's territory the
knowledge of any threatening movement by
a neighbour. Takeda Shingen, for example,
established a complex network of fire
beacons across Kai, so that any move by his
great rival Uesugi Kenshin could be notified
to his capital at Kofu as quickly as possible.
The beacons were maintained in wooden
towers. Combustible material kept ready in a
bucket was lighted and swung up into the air
on a long pivoting arm. Once the nature and

severity of the threat had been assessed, a
call to arms could begin among the part-time
soldiers and farmers through the
communication medium of a runner, a bell
or a conch shell trumpet. The troops would
then report to the nearest castle.

## Verbal and written communications

When a samurai army was on the march,
scouts would be sent on ahead to report back
on enemy movements. Sometimes a scouting
operation would take the form of a
'reconnaissance in force', with the unit
deliberately coming to grips with the enemy
ranks to test their mettle. The men chosen
for this vital task were always both excellent
horsemen and brave fighters, and their
exploits are celebrated in chronicles such as
*Hojo Godaiki*, where the bravery of the horses
is also commended in one incident when
two Hojo scouts were surrounded and
almost captured.

Messages from the scouts would be
delivered to the *daimyo* at great personal risk
to the messenger, and could be either verbal
or written. A good example of verbal
communications from scouts is the battle of
Chiksan in Korea in 1597. Here the advance
guard came upon a large Chinese army and
sent scouts back to the main body while the
rest of the force engaged the enemy to buy
time; in fact the sound of firing transferred
the gist of their message much more quickly
than did the galloping horsemen. It is also
interesting to note that many surviving
letters containing official information end
with the words: 'You will be informed of
these things by the messenger.' This was in
case the written message was intercepted by
the enemy.

During sieges, written messages were
delivered over the walls of a castle by the
time-honoured method of the arrow letter, a
device noted frequently during the siege of
Hara castle in 1638, although there existed
actual signalling arrows that had a hollow,
turnip-shaped wooden head and whistled as

they flew through the air. These were traditionally used at the start of a battle and were regarded as a call to the gods to witness the brave deeds that were about to take place. During the 12th century signal arrows began the archery duel between mounted samurai bowmen, but by the Sengoku Period this procedure had long since been replaced by hundreds of ashigaru firing a volley of arquebus bullets.

The messengers on a battlefield were drawn from the same elite samurai ranks as the scouts but had the more restricted role of communication between friendly troops rather than intelligence gathering. They had to be very easily recognised in the heat and smoke of battle, so were often distinguished by a *horo*, a cloak stretched over a basketwork frame. The *horo* would often bear the *daimyo*'s *mon* (badge) on a brightly coloured background, and when the *horo* filled up with air as the horsemen rode along, his master's colours were recognisable from a considerable distance. There is a reference in the *Hosokawa Yusai Oboegaki* to the elite status of a *horo* wearer and the following recommendation:

*When taking the head of a horo warrior wrap it in the silk of the horo, and in the case of an ordinary warrior, wrap it in the silk of the sashimono.*

## Visible communication devices

During the Sengoku Period we see the widespread and systematic use of coloured flags to denote subunits of an army. In addition to the *hata jirushi* (streamers), which had been in use for centuries, we begin to see considerable numbers of *nobori* – long, narrow, vertical flags kept rigid by a short cross-pole so that the flag would not wrap round the shaft in a wind and therefore become unidentifiable. *Nobori* were most commonly used for indicating subdivisions within an army or simply for providing a grand heraldic display using scores of identical banners.

While *nobori* and the older style of *hata jirushi* provided overall identification and organisation, another type of flag was introduced to give units of samurai spearmen and swordsmen a more prominent visual appearance. This was the *sashimono*, the most important heraldic innovation introduced during the Sengoku Period. Most *sashimono* consisted of a small flag made rigid by two poles threaded through the cloth. The flag was flown from a lacquered wooden carrying shaft, securely fastened to the back of the armour and held in place by the two ends of a cord that passed under the armpits and were tied on to the metal rings on the samurai's breastplate. The *sashimono* would often bear the *daimyo*'s *mon*, making the whole army look uniform, with units being distinguished from one another by the colour of the field of the flag. With so many flags now appearing on a battlefield, the *daimyo*'s own identification had to be more prominent than ever, and the most spectacular sight were the *uma jirushi* (literally 'horse insignia'), which were the *daimyo*'s standards. They were sometimes large rectangular or long *nobori*-type flags, but were more usually huge three-dimensional objects in the shape of bells, umbrellas, gongs or streamers.

The most important visual signalling device of all was the general's war fan. His subordinate officers would watch to see the fan being lowered in the general's hand to indicate an attack and its general direction. There were three types in common use: a bundle of oiled paper tassels hanging from a short shaft, a recognisable fan that was of paper on metal spokes, and a rigid wooden or metal fan that resembled the ones used nowadays by sumo wrestling referees. The command transferred from the general by his fan was then communicated further afield by various visual and audible signalling devices.

A warrior wearing a *horo*, the curious stiffened cloak commonly worn by messengers and bodyguards to increase their visibility. This samurai has received an arrow through his arm.

## Audible communication devices

The most important audible communication devices were drums, conch shell trumpets and bells. Drums had been a feature of battlefield life since ancient times, and provided the means of raising an army's morale as well as being used for mere communication and signalling, and all castles would have a drum tower. Drums could also be used for time-keeping in camp, although this was a function more usually

noted for bells and conches; their most important role was that of stimulating an army and controlling the speed of its pace on active service. Many of the later chronicles stress the importance of using drums to control an army's movements on campaign and on the battlefield. Japanese armies marched to the beat of a drum, and on the march the *taiko yaku* (drummer) would set the pace. It was customary for the army to march in step with the drum, with six paces taken between each beat. In practical terms this probably meant a rhythm of beat-2-3-4-5-6; beat-2-3-4-5-6, so that the beat was always struck on the same foot. By the middle of the Sengoku Period set drum calls existed for advancing and retreating in battle. The *Hojo Godaiki* tells us:

*If battle plans have been put into disorder, the soldiers hear the blowing of the conch, and similarly the drum and they withdraw.*

The *Gunji Yoshu* gives more details on drum calls. To summon one's allies the drum call was nine sets of five beats at an appropriate pace, and:

*When advancing one's own troops and pursuing an enemy [the call is] nine sets of three beats, speeded up three or four times, and the giving of a war cry. As for the number of war cries, shout 'Ei! Ei! O!' twice.*

Just as for marching, the drummer would beat the drum faster to speed up an army's pace in attack. As the *Gunji Yoshu* puts it:

*Having become a victorious army, to mop up the enemy you are pursuing, the drum is beaten more and more'. The sound had the effect of disheartening the pursued as well as encouraging the pursuers, and the same chronicle suggests ringing the camp bell faster and faster as well to add to the effect.*

Small hand-drums do not appear to have been used at all in a military context. Instead all illustrations depict drums that are either mounted on a static framework or carried by

someone other than the drummer. Larger ones appear to have been slung on a pole between two men's shoulders, while a more common and smaller version was carried on one man's back while another did the beating. These drums could either be secured by simple cords, as in the two examples depicted on the Nagashino Screen, or mounted on elaborate wooden carrying frames.

The conch shell trumpet has a history as long as that of the drum in Japanese warfare. It was a large conch shell with a bronze metal mouthpiece attached, slung in an openwork cord basket and carried by the *kai yaku* (trumpeter). Apart from its military use, the conch was closely associated with the yamabushi, the adherents of the religious sect of Shugendo, who carried out ascetic practices in mountains. The conch shell trumpet was a feature of a yamabushi pilgrim's equipment, and records exist of *daimyo* recruiting experienced yamabushi conch blowers into their ranks to act as trumpeters.

The conch performed a similar function to the drum for imposing a rhythm on an army and, in particular, provided something of a 'heroic musical accompaniment' to battlefield endeavour. However, it was also used for signalling, and a complex system of conch trumpet calls existed. Used in conjunction with the bell, the *jinkai* (war conch) was employed for establishing troop formations, and all ranks were expected to know and recognise the different calls.

Unlike the conch and the drum, the bell was not usually a portable signalling device; if a bell was used on the battlefield, it would be mounted next to the general's headquarters post. Its use was also more restricted than the other two instruments, although it could be used to encourage soldiers to advance. There is a reference for the Uesugi family of the bell used in an almost identical manner to the conch in making the army ready for action. In the Uesugi case, the first bell meant stop eating or do not start. The second bell meant put on your armour, while the third was the signal for departure. In each case the bell was rung once, rather than the complex patterns of conch blows, and in this the bell made up for its lack of portability, with its sonorous reverberations that could carry quite a distance. One chronicle of the Korean War notes a bell echoing from a tower in an area bounded on all sides by hills. This made it very effective for conveying signals. During the Edo Period this same quality of the bell was put to use as warnings to the inhabitants of a city of an outbreak of fire.

During the Gempei War in the 12th century we read of armies communicating by using temple bells, but as these were too heavy to transport to a battlefield they were replaced by bells of about half the size. One of these, used in war by the Takeda, is now preserved as an actual temple bell at Kawanakajima. Bells were of bronze, and were rung by striking them from outside with a wooden hammer rather than with an internal suspended clapper. A bell in an army's ranks could give a very prominent and farreaching announcement of an enemy attack, but they were not used for giving orders to advance or retreat on a battlefield; that was left to the drums and conches. There is however a reference to an action in 1560 when a bell called the samurai back to the castle, but this was a pre-arranged signal to use in an emergency.

Gongs (*dora* in Japanese) provided a lighter alternative, and their sonority was brought out by beating them with a thick rope. The final signalling devices were the *hyoshigi* (wooden clappers), which consisted simply of two wooden blocks tied together and one being struck by the other. They were used for time-keeping in cities during the Edo Period and in a similar role within an army camp during the Sengoku Period, where they would be carried on policing duties. However, they had a very short range and had no use on a battlefield.

# The age of fission

The wars of the Sengoku Period happened along two dimensions. The first was the dimension of time, and the previous chapter showed how this affected the development of weaponry and tactics. The history of the fighting that went on may also be approached through the processes of fission and fusion. The former involved wars breaking out following the collapse of central authority in the Onin War; this created individual *daimyo* who then fought one another. The process of fusion covers the creation of a new central authority by Oda Nobunaga, Toyotomi Hideyoshi and Tokugawa Ieyasu. As noted earlier, there is a considerable overlap between the two processes, because Nobunaga's initial progress towards unity consisted to a large extent of consolidating his own territory and adding to it just like any other Sengoku *daimyo*.

The other dimension is that of space, because until the process of reunification was well under way, particularly that phase of it associated with Hideyoshi, geographically separate areas of Japan were left to their own devices,. This meant, for example, that the wars between the Takeda, Uesugi and Hojo in the Kanto bore no relation to what was happening among the *daimyo* of Kyushu. It was only from the mid-1580s, when massive armies existed and could be moved around the country with ease, that the fate of one area began to depend upon the fate of another.

Nevertheless, the processes by which the fighting began through fission were remarkably similar throughout Japan, and one family in particular provides an excellent introduction. No fewer than five generations of the Hojo family of Odawara formed an unbroken succession from the Onin War to Hideyoshi's reunification in 1590, during which time they fought some of Japan's most celebrated battles and grew in stature and number in a way that was almost incredible. For this reason we will trace the history of the five generations of the Hojo and their century of fission as a way of providing an overview of this process within the Sengoku Period.

## The first generation: Hojo Soun

The way in which the founder of the Hojo seized his opportunity amidst the general lawlessness of the times provides a fascinating illustration of how a 'little war' of the Sengoku Period could break out. The Hojo had had a very modest beginning, when, within a few years of the end of the Onin War, an obscure samurai had begun laying the foundations of this family's future greatness in what was to become a classic model of Sengoku warfare. In 1480 Ise Shinkuro Nagauji had only six men under his command. By the time of the death of his great-great grandson in 1590, that original war band had grown to tens of thousands, who defended their territory from formidable castles.

Ise Shinkuro, or Hojo Soun, as he is known to history, has often been portrayed as a very lowly samurai, or even a *ronin* (a warrior unemployed because of the death or disgrace of his master), but in fact Soun had very respectable family connections. He was born in 1432, and his elder sister had married Imagawa Yoshitada from an illustrious family in Suruga province. When Yoshitada was killed in battle in 1480 his son Ujichika's rightful inheritance was placed in great peril, so Ise Shinkuro went to his assistance with the aforementioned six men. His military skills settled the matter, and the grateful heir rewarded him with a castle. In 1493 Soun was provided with a further opportunity to

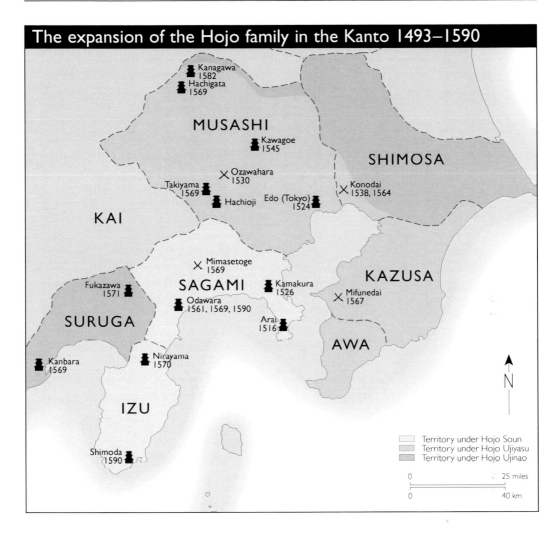

## The expansion of the Hojo family in the Kanto 1493–1590

Kanagawa
1582
Hachigata
1569

MUSASHI

Kawagoe
1545

SHIMOSA

× Ozawahara
1530

Takiyama
1569

Konodai
1538, 1564

Hachioji    Edo (Tokyo)
1524

KAI

× Mimasetoge
1569

Fukazawa
1571

SAGAMI    Kamakura
1526

KAZUSA

Mifunedai
1567

Odawara
1561, 1569, 1590

Arai
1516

SURUGA

Kanbara
1569

Nirayama
1570

AWA

N

IZU

Shimoda
1590

Territory under Hojo Soun
Territory under Hojo Ujiyasu
Territory under Hojo Ujinao

0                    25 miles

0                    40 km

The Hojo dominated the affairs of the Kanto area for almost a century. This map shows how their territories expanded from the time of the seizure of Izu by the first daimyo Hojo Soun, through the successful reign of the third-generation Hojo Ujiyasu, until the destruction of the fifth and last *daimyo*, Hojo Ujinao, in 1590.

benefit through righting wrongs. A certain Chachamaru, a young man who had not yet received his adult name and was the nephew of the shogun Yoshimasa, of silver temple fame, was dispossessed and ordered by his father to enter a monastery. Chachamaru responded by murdering his stepmother and brother-in-law, so the ever helpful Ise Soun went to war and destroyed Chachamaru. With the support of those who had welcomed the move, Soun added the Ashikaga's Izu province to his own territories.

The following year Soun acquired for the Hojo the site that was to be the family's future capital, Odawara, on Sagami Bay. The story of Soun's capture of Odawara is somewhat unsavoury but not untypical of the age: he allegedly arranged for the castle's young lord to be murdered while out hunting. In 1512 Kamakura, the ancient shogunal capital, was also added to the Hojo territories, followed by Arai castle in 1518, famous for the defiant suicide of the defeated lord Miura Yoshimoto, who cut off his own head! Soun's subsequent change of name from Ise to Hojo was done to associate his new and powerful family in this part of Japan with the earlier Hojo of Kamakura, who had ruled Japan as regents for 150 years. It was the Kamakura Hojo who had repelled the

Mongol invasions. The new Hojo (who are often called the Odawara Hojo) also helped themselves to the Kamakura Hojo's *mon*.

## The second generation: Hojo Ujitsuna

Hojo Soun was succeeded by his son Hojo Ujitsuna, who continued his father's programme of conquest. In 1524 Ujitsuna led an army against Edo castle, which lay in the centre of the important rice-growing area of the Kanto plain. Edo castle is now the Imperial Palace in Tokyo, but at that time it was an ordinary castle guarding a fishing village, and its owner, Uesugi Tomooki of the Ogigayatsu branch of the family, was most reluctant to give it up to the Hojo. In fact Uesugi took the initiative by marching his troops out to stop the Hojo advance at an important river crossing called Takanawa, but Hojo Ujitsuna cleverly bypassed him and assaulted the Uesugi from the rear. Tomooki then retreated to Edo, only to find that the castle keeper, Ota Suketada, was in secret communication with the Hojo and had opened the gates to them.

The loss of Edo to the Hojo set in motion 17 years of war between the Uesugi and the Hojo for control of the Kanto, and the initiative continued to swing from one side to the other and back again. In 1526 Uesugi's ally Satomi Sanetaka scored a notable triumph over the Hojo when he captured Kamakura from them and burned to the ground the great Tsurugaoka Hachiman shrine. This was a very symbolic loss, because it was in Kamakura that the earlier Hojo had committed suicide en masse when the city had fallen in 1333. Soon the Hojo had rivals on their western flank as well, because when Imagawa Yoshimoto succeeded to the headship of the Imagawa in Suruga province, he turned his back on the service once provided to his ancestors by Soun, and made an alliance with the Takeda against the Hojo.

The Uesugi came back into the fray in 1535, when Tomooki noticed the absence of Hojo Ujitsuna from his home province (he was busy fighting the Takeda) and invaded

Hojo territories, but Ujitsuna managed to return in time, and defeated the Uesugi at Iruma. Tomooki died in his castle of Kawagoe in 1537 and was succeeded by Uesugi Tomosada. Guessing that the Uesugi would be in some disarray, Hojo Ujitsuna attacked and captured Kawagoe, and the Hojo finally had the key to the Kanto.

Shimosa province, which lay just round Tokyo Bay, was their next objective. Opposing the Hojo in 1537 was an allied army of Ashikaga Yoshiaki and Satomi Yoshitaka, who was based at his castle of Konodai. Ashikaga Yoshiaki was advised by his allies to attack the Hojo before they had a chance to cross the Tonegawa river towards him. The over-confident Yoshiaki, however, refused to move, but it soon became obvious that the Hojo were driving his men back. Satomi Yoshitaka then descended from Konodai hill, along with Yoshiaki's eldest son Motoyori. With his comrades being killed all around him, Motoyori stood steadfast and killed 30 of the Hojo samurai before being overcome himself. When the news of the death of his son reached Yoshiaki, he went mad with rage and spurred his horse; under his furious leadership the whole trend of the battle of Konodai was reversed until Yoshiaki was forced to pause for breath. An archer from the Hojo ranks recognised his heraldry and put a shaft into his chest. With his death, the advantage immediately returned to the Hojo side, and the victory of Konodai was theirs.

## The third generation: Hojo Ujiyasu

Before he died, in 1540, Hojo Ujitsuna completed the rebuilding of Kamakura, making it, together with Odawara and Edo, into a symbol of the growing power of the Hojo. Their third generation was represented by Hojo Ujiyasu, generally regarded as the finest of the five Hojo *daimyo*. He was also the contemporary of Uesugi Kenshin, Takeda Shingen and Imagawa Yoshimoto, all of whom kept the Hojo armies very busy during his long reign.

The death of a leader was always a signal for rivals to try their luck, and when Ogigayatsu Tomosada heard of the death of Ujitsuna, he tried unsuccessfully to recapture Edo castle. In 1545, having had more time to prepare, Tomosada allied himself with Ashikaga Haruuji and, taking along Uesugi Norimasa from the other Uesugi branch, he marched against Kawagoe castle, defended by Ujiyasu's brother Hojo Tsunanari. Despite a garrison only 3,000 strong, Tsunanari managed to hold out against 85,000 besiegers. Hojo Ujiyasu marched to Kawagoe's relief with 8,000 soldiers, and a brave samurai managed to slip past the Uesugi siege lines to tell his brother that they were on their way. The relief force was another pitifully small army, but so confident was Ujiyasu that he offered a deal to Ashikaga Haruuji, whom he perceived as the weakest of the allies. His offer was rejected, but intelligence brought back from the allied lines by a ninja suggested that the besiegers were so confident of victory that their vigilance had slackened.

Ujiyasu decided to make a night attack – a risky tactic at any time, but it was to be coordinated with a sortie from the castle by Tsunanari. To help matters further, Ujiyasu issued orders that his men should not overburden themselves by wearing heavy armour, and, most surprising of all, that no one was to waste time taking heads. This great samurai tradition was a time-consuming process that involved identifying the victim and noting the name of the victor – clearly inappropriate during a night attack. It says a great deal for the loyalty of the Hojo samurai that they willingly suspended this most basic of samurai privileges for the common good. The plans worked perfectly, and with the odds of ten to one against them the Hojo triumphed. The coalition against them was utterly destroyed, and Hojo control over the Kanto was dramatically confirmed.

The victory of Kawagoe also meant the extinction of the two branches of the Uesugi family, and the next we hear of an Uesugi going into battle is in the person of Uesugi Kenshin, who, like the Hojo, changed his name to something formerly illustrious. In Kenshin's case he obtained the name from the last of the line who had been defeated by the Hojo and sought refuge with him. As Uesugi Kenshin, this new force on the scene marched against the Hojo in 1561 and laid siege to Odawara castle, but after two months of fighting he could make no impression on it and he withdrew when the Takeda threatened his own territories. Two years later Hojo Ujiyasu and Takeda Shingen were to be found as allies besieging Uesugi's castle of Musashi-Matsuyama, just one more example of the shifting alliances during these turbulent times.

In 1564 a succession dispute pitted the Hojo against the Satomi once more, and history was repeated when Satomi Yoshihiro began an advance against the Hojo. Ujiyasu responded, and the two met in battle at Konodai, where Hojo Ujiyasu's father Ujitsuna had defeated Yoshihiro's father Yoshitaka in 1537. This time the Hojo were by far the stronger force, with 20,000 troops to the Satomi's 8,000. In Ujiyasu's orders to his men there appeared the confident phrase: 'It will be a short battle, so do not bring labourers along.' Not surprisingly, the Satomi drew back when the superior numbers of the Hojo vanguard attacked, but this was an illusion, because the Satomi were trying to trap them with a false retreat. However, Ujiyasu was too cunning to be caught like that, and had sent his son and heir Ujimasa in an encircling movement to the Satomi rear. Satomi Yoshihiro was trapped, but taking his sword in his hands he broke through the Hojo line, only to see his 15-year-old son Chokuro killed by the Hojo retainer Matsuda Yasuyoshi. As happened to others in samurai history, Matsuda felt remorse at having killed a young boy, and left the battlefield to live as a priest for the rest of his life. Hojo Ujiyasu expressed his emotions at winning the battle and gaining Konodai castle in his own way. He set up his camp stool on the edge of Konodai hill above the river, and composed a poem.

*Conquering the foe*
*As I wished at Konodai*
*Now do I behold*
*The evening sunshine of Katsuura*

One of the greatest assets that Hojo Ujiyasu possessed was seven fine sons, and two of them were to earn glory for themselves in 1569 when, with their former alliance now sundered, the mighty Takeda Shingen moved against the Hojo. The campaign, which finished with the battle of Mimasetoge, one of the few examples in Japanese history of a battle fought on a mountain, provided Hojo Ujiyasu with the last and strongest challenge of his reign. Shingen's army entered Musashi province out of Kai and first laid siege to Hachigata castle, defended by Ujiyasu's third son Ujikuni. They failed to capture the castle, and moved on to Takiyama, held by the second son, Ujiteru, where they were similarly repulsed. To carry on from there to Odawara, with two intact fortresses behind him, was a surprising decision for the experienced Takeda Shingen, and he certainly seems to have outreached himself. His resulting siege of Odawara only lasted three days, after which he burned the castle town outside Odawara and withdrew.

Subsequent events strongly indicate that Hojo Ujiyasu quickly realised that he had been given an excellent opportunity for a decisive showdown with the Takeda. He also appreciated that this would have to be done in the mountains if the Hojo were not to face the famous Takeda cavalry on the flat plains of Musashi province. The plan was for Ujiteru and Ujikuni to ambush the Takeda as they made their way home through the pass of Mimasetoge. This was carried out, and may well have succeeded until, after a day of fighting, Yamagata Masakage, one of the Takeda's most experienced generals, launched a devastating flank attack on the Hojo left wing. The main body of the Takeda then broke through and escaped to Kofu.

## The fourth generation: Hojo Ujimasa

Hojo Ujiyasu died in 1570, and the fourth *daimyo*, Hojo Ujimasa, was to find himself as busy with diplomatic negotiations as his father had been with fighting. This was the decade that also saw the deaths of Takeda Shingen and Uesugi Kenshin and the notable victories of Anegawa and Nagashino by Oda Nobunaga. Secure behind the Hakone mountains, Hojo Ujimasa could watch while Nobunaga fought Takeda Katsuyori and the Ikko-ikki. The Hojo stayed well out of these matters, but when Nobunaga was murdered and Hideyoshi took over his domains, the balance of power in Japan began to change. When Shikoku and Kyushu islands were added to Hideyoshi's territories, the Hojo began to wonder if their mountain passes and strong castles of the Kanto would be likely to hold back Hideyoshi.

## The fifth generation: Hojo Ujinao

The final challenge came in 1590. Ujimasa abdicated in favour of the fifth *daimyo*, Hojo Ujinao, and it was he who was to experience the largest besieging operation ever carried out in Japan up to that time. As if to mock the Hojo, Hideyoshi's army effectively built a 'siege city' rather than siege lines, round Odawara, where they entertained dancing girls and feasted loudly. There was some military activity – just enough to let the Hojo know that their besiegers could fight as well as they could drink – but the inevitable end was a negotiated surrender. The conditions of capitulation included the suicide of the retired *daimyo* Hojo Ujimasa, the banishment of the current *daimyo*, Ujinao, and the suicide of Ujimasa's brother Ujiteru. The acts of *hara kiri* were performed within the keep of Odawara, and five generations of the most consistently successful Sengoku *daimyo* came to a final and bloody end. They had lasted a century, and in this particular area of Japan, although later than almost anywhere else, an entirely new process of fusion was about to begin.

# Samurai at war

## Part I: The fission continues

The above account of the Hojo shows how war broke out in one area of Japan and continued for almost a century until reunification began. This was a pattern repeated across the country, and is a topic that can only be dealt with adequately on a geographical basis.

### Central Japan: Kawanakajima

The borders of the Hojo territories touched those of Uesugi Kenshin and Takeda Shingen, some of whose battles were noted above, but these two rivals are most renowned in Japanese history because they fought no fewer than five battles in the same place within a period of ten years. The place was Kawanakajima, and the fighting varied from impressive stalemates to at least one massive encounter, the fourth battle of Kawanakajima, in 1561. This produced among the largest percentage casualty figures for any battle of the Sengoku Period.

The strategy adopted by Takeda Shingen was to flush out the Uesugi troops by a surprise night raid on the rear of the hill where they had taken up their position. Once down on the plain and disorganised, the renowned Takeda cavalry would be able to ride them down at ease. However, Uesugi Kensin learned of the plan and brought his army down from the hill before the Takeda launched their raid. While Takeda Shingen was still ignorant of what had happened, the Uesugi came looming out of the early morning mist in a surprise attack of their own against the Takeda lines. So great was the shock that the Uesugi vanguard broke through as far as the Takeda headquarters troops and Shingen's bodyguard, where the two commanders are believed to have fought a single combat.

### Western Japan: the battle of the holy island

Elsewhere in Japan the fighting of the Sengoku Period was also well under way. Far to the west, on the shores of the Inland Sea, lay the lands of Ouchi Yoshitaka, who was the exact opposite of Hojo Soun. He was no opportunist, but an aristocrat whose family had served the shogun for generations. Following the collapse of that admirable institution, he had proceeded to safeguard the best interests of the local inhabitants by ruling them himself. Naturally this involved wars with neighbours, but it was through the machinations of one of his own retainers, who took the Hojo Soun role, that the nemesis of the Ouchi finally came.

The retainer's name was Sue Harukata, and his was one typical means of becoming a Sengoku *daimyo*. Harukata revolted against his lord and seized his domains in a coup. However, Ouchi had other retainers, and one of them, Mori Motonari, set out to avenge his late master. The key to their rival strategic positions was the holy island of Miyajima, where the Shinto religion decreed that neither birth nor death should take place. Mori Motonari made a great show of fortifying Miyajima, which he then allowed Sue Harukata to capture. His enemy was now cornered on this tiny scrap of land, so one dark night Mori Motonari launched an amphibious operation and caught the Sue army off guard.

As a result the Mori family grew to be the Hojo of western Japan. Many local campaigns followed, particularly against the Amako family, helped by the Mori's skilled use of their sea power among the mass of tiny islands that dotted the coast. They also came to grips with the Otomo family of nearby Kyushu island, when they contested the castle of Moji, which occupied a prominent vantage point overlooking the straits of Shimonoseki. Moji changed hands between the Otomo and the Mori five times between 1557 and 1561, in spite of gunfire, amphibious assault and even a bombardment from Portuguese ships. The latter was a unique event in Japanese history, and provided a dramatic illustration of the devastating effects of cannonballs against a mainly wooden fortress.

## Southern Japan: the early Kyushu wars

The Otomo family of Kyushu, whom the Mori fought at Moji, were one of the strongest *daimyo* families in southern Japan, but as in so many cases during the Sengoku Period a *daimyo*'s complacency proved to be his undoing. The Otomo *daimyo* gives us an example of this during another classic account of a night battle in 1570, when his army was surprised during a celebration.

The above examples of the collapse of shogunal authority followed by territorial expansion at the expense of one's neighbours may be seen in Kyushu as everywhere else in Japan. In 1570 the *daimyo* Otomo Sorin's objective was the territory of Ryuzoji Takanobu in Chikuzen province, and Sorin had appointed his son Chikasada as commanding general to lay siege to Saga castle. Saga had a garrison of only 5,000 men against Otomo's probable 60,000, an estimated figure brought to the Ryuzoji's emergency council of war by scouts. The Otomo army was spread in a huge arc round Saga, anchored at each end on the sea coast. The scouts also brought the intelligence that Otomo Chikasada was planning to hold some form of celebration inside his field headquarters that night, prior to attacking Saga the following morning. The base was located on the hill of Imayama, about four miles north-west of Saga castle, and 3,000 of his bodyguard were there with him.

Samurai field headquarters were never very elaborate – usually an enclosed space defined by the *maku* (field curtains) that were set off with the *daimyo*'s *mon*. To Nabeshima Naoshige, Ryuzoji's leading

retainer and a man who would one day become a *daimyo* in his own right, it was an ideal target for a night raid, but most of his colleagues did not agree. It was apparently Ryuzoji Takanobu's mother who shamed them into following Nabeshima's advice with the words: 'Isn't your attitude towards the enemy forces like a mouse in front of a cat? If you are real samurai then carry out Nobushige's night raid on the Otomo headquarters. Decide between life or death and victory or defeat!'

That night a detachment of Ryuzoji samurai and footsoldiers silently approached the curtained area on the lower slopes of Imayama hill, keeping their advantage of height, and waited until dawn. The Otomo troops had clearly enjoyed their pre-battle party, and were sleeping off the effects of the sake (rice wine). Even the guards must have been lulled into a false sense of security by their own overwhelming numbers, because we are told that without any warning, Nabeshima Naoshige ordered his arquebusiers to open fire, and 800 samurai charged down into the position. They first put out all the Otomo's pine torches, the only illumination before the sun rose, and then began to extinguish the Otomo samurai. It was a massacre: Otomo Chikasada was cut down, and 2,000 out of the 3,000 men in the headquarters area were also killed. Taking advantage of the confusion, Ryuzoji Takanobu led another attack out of the castle against a different section of the siege lines. So devastating was the night raid that Otomo Sorin withdrew the rest of his troops and left the Ryuzoji well alone.

## Southern Japan: the battle of Okita Nawate

The Ryuzoji consolidated their position in north-west Kyushu over the next decade, but this was the Sengoku Period, and the balance of power was changing all the time. The Otomo were still a force to be reckoned with in north-east Kyushu, but a tremendous new power was rising in the south in the shape of the Shimazu family of Satsuma, who forced the Otomo to stay within their territories in the decisive battle of Mimigawa in 1578, which left thousands of dying Otomo samurai strewn along the banks of the river.

Among the smaller *daimyo* families still left in Kyushu by the 1580s were the Arima of the Shimabara peninsula in Hizen province. Like other *daimyo* of similar power and influence elsewhere in Japan, Arima

Ryuzoji Takenobu, one of the sengoku *daimyo* from the island of Kyushu. His family rose to prominence as a result of the battle of Iwayama in 1570.

Harunobu was being harassed by a powerful
neighbour, in this case Ryuzoji Takanobu,
and felt compelled to turn to an even bigger
neighbour, the Shimazu, for assistance. Such
a request provided an excellent opportunity
for the Shimazu to inflict defeat upon a
major rival, so in spite of objections from
some of his retainers, Shimazu Yoshihisa sent
a force of 3,000 soldiers, under Shimazu
Iehisa, across Shimabara Bay to the peninsula
of Shimabara. Taking the bait, Ryuzoji
Takanobu marched down to Shimabara at
the head of 50,000 men, and the two sides
met in a fierce battle at Okita Nawate, about
a mile north of Shimabara, in March 1584.

The battle was fought in an area between
the seashore and the wooded mountains
along the line of a rough road. Ryuzoji
Takanobu divided his force into three for an
advance against Shimabara beside the
wooded hills, along the road and by the
seashore. The Shimazu and Arima forces took
up sensible defensive positions and closed
off the approaches to Shimabara by building
a brushwood palisade that stretched down to
the sea. Through this a hastily erected but
very solid wooden gate gave access to the
road. The land around was swampy, so the
Shimazu were well protected. Their
intentions were to put in place a tactic that
had become almost a trademark of the
Shimazu: a spirited attack that was then
converted into a false retreat, against which
the enemy would advance at his peril and be
engulfed in turn. The Shimazu centre was
held by Shimazu Iehisa, with a 50-man
strong vanguard unit under Akaboshi
Nobuiie, whose family had been taken
hostage by the Ryuzoji; they could be relied
upon to attack with great vigour. A detached
Shimazu force lay concealed in the woods on
the landward side, while the Arima provided
unusual flank support in the shape of a
floating gunnery line of arquebus squads of
30 men in each of 13 boats. They kept up a
fierce fire against the Ryuzoji from offshore
with heavy calibre arquebuses and two
cannon – probably breech-loading swivel
guns. The fact that Arima Harunobu was one
of the few Christian *daimyo* could not fail to

The black cross in a ring indicates that these fellows are
Shimazu samurai in action. The Shimazu of Satsuma were
defeated by Toyotomi Hideyoshi in 1587.

attract the attention of the Jesuit Luis Frois,
who described the bombardment:

*The rhythm to which they kept was really
something to see. First of all, reverently kneeling
down with their hands towards heaven, they
began reciting, 'Our Father which art in heaven,
hallowed be thy name ...' The first phase of the*

*strategy being thus completed, they turned impatiently to load the cannon balls, and fired with such force against the enemy that with only one shot the whole sky could be seen to be filled with limbs. They fell on their knees once more. The petitions of the Sunday oration followed and in this way they inflicted heavy losses on the pagans, who lacked the courage to advance.*

In spite of the casualties from the Arima guns, Ryuzoji had drawn the conclusion that the Shimazu force in the centre was small enough to be overcome easily. Waving his war fan, he led an advance down the road against the gate in the palisade to the accompaniment of loud war cries. Their front ranks were then attacked by the fanatics of Akaboshi, and the Ryuzoji were driven back by the fury of the assault. They collided with their comrades advancing behind them, and such was the confusion that Ryuzoji Takanobu sent a messenger to find out what was going on. The reply that reached him drew him to the conclusion

The site of the battle of Okita Nawate on the Shimabara peninsula in 1584, where Ryuzoji Takanobu was killed, taking the fate of his family with him.

that the advance should continue, but in the melee his troops inevitably spilled out on both sides of the road, where they came under fire from bows and arquebuses shooting from behind the rough palisade, just as at the battle of Nagashino. At that point Shimazu Iehisa flung open the gate on the Shimabara road, and the Satsuma samurai charged forward in classic style. They burst through three ranks of the Ryuzoji and reached Takanobu's bodyguard, who were powerless to save their lord, and a Shimazu retainer called Kawakami Tadatoshi took his head. So died the 'Bear of Hizen' as he was nicknamed, at the age of 56, and there was now one less *daimyo* in Kyushu.

## Part II: The age of fusion

It would be possible to fill this entire book with battle stories similar to the above, but this would be misleading, because the

process of fusion that succeeded the process of fission was already under way, and it is to this important topic that we must now turn.

### The rise of Oda Nobunaga

The above excursion into Kyushu took us forward three decades from the glory days of the Mori and the Uesugi. Now we must go back to central Japan and the year 1560, when the process of fusion was about to begin. Here we meet the first of the three great unifiers of Japan: Oda Nobunaga, a minor *daimyo* living in a province adjacent to the territories of one of Japan's most powerful *daimyo*, Imagawa Yoshimoto.

By the year 1560 there existed several Sengoku *daimyo* like Hojo Ujiyasu and Takeda Shingen, who possessed the military resources to begin the reunification of Japan, but in nearly every case political or geographical factors meant that they had to concentrate instead on maintaining their own territories against their neighbours. Imagawa Yoshimoto was different. The location of his domains along the line of the Tokaido, the Eastern Sea Road, gave him a considerable advantage when it came to

Oda Nobunaga, the first of the three great unifiers of Japan,
from a painted scroll.

# The campaigns of Oda Nobunaga and Toyotomi Hideyoshi 1560–85

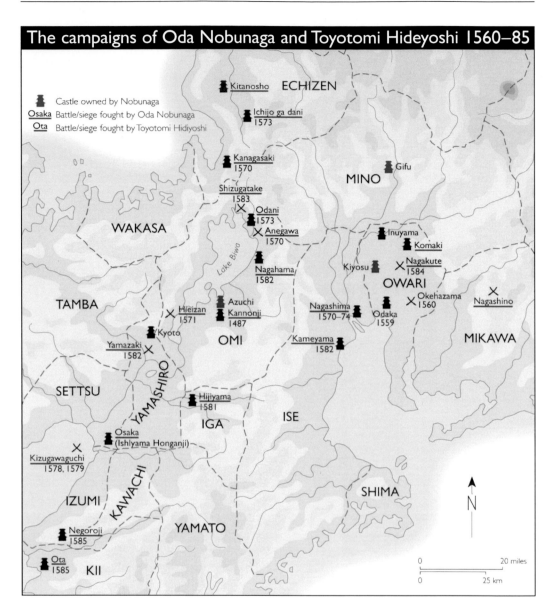

Nobunaga's castles and battles. from his triumph at Okehazama to his death at the Honnoji temple in Kyoto in 1582. We also see Toyotomi Hideyoshi's revenge for Nobunaga at Yamazaki in 1582, the Shizugatake campaign of 1583 and his conflict with Tokugawa Ieyasu at Komaki-Nagakute.

considerable advantage when it came to communications, so in 1560 he prepared to advance on Kyoto to make the latest shogun bend to his will.

His first objective was the province of Owari, which was ruled by the minor *daimyo* Oda Nobunaga, whose army the Imagawa

outnumbered by 12 to 1. At first all went well, and the Oda border fortresses tumbled before the Imagawa advance, but Yoshimoto grew complacent and took a break to perform the traditional head-viewing ceremony in a small wooded ravine called Okehazama. Young Oda Nobunaga seized his chance, and attacked the Imagawa encampment under the cover of a fortuitous thunderstorm. Before Yoshimoto knew what was happening, his head had been lopped off his shoulders. The brief battle of Okehazama put paid to all the Imagawa

Nobunaga to the first rank of samurai
commanders. The time of fusion had begun.

Eight years were to pass before Oda
Nobunaga attempted his own march on
Kyoto, and in this time he consolidated his
own position, made allies and fought wars
just like any other Sengoku *daimyo*. The
immediate response to his victory over the
Imagawa was a large number of desertions
from the Imagawa camp, and many of these
former allies saw a better future for
themselves allied to Oda Nobunaga.
Tokugawa Ieyasu, who was to become the
third of the great unifiers, was the most
notable *daimyo* in this category. Of
Nobunaga's military conquests, the most
significant was the taking of Inabayama
(Gifu) castle from the Saito in 1567. With
Gifu as his base, and with Tokugawa
providing his rearguard along the Tokaido,
Nobunaga entered Kyoto in 1568 and
deposed the last Ashikaga shogun, Yoshiaki.

Oda Nobunaga's capture of Kyoto was a
significant and very symbolic step. All the
other great *daimyo* felt that Nobunaga had
stolen a march upon them. The main local
opposition to this important development in
Japanese politics came from the Asai and
Asakura families, who threatened Nobunaga
from the north, and the various coteries
of warrior monks who were to engage
Nobunaga in war for the next 12 years. Oda

The death of Imagawa Yoshimoto at the battle of
Okehazama in 1560. This was the victory that launched
Oda Nobunaga on his path to greatness.

Nobunaga won the victory of Anegawa
against the Asai and Asakura in 1570. This
was a fierce encounter fought in blazing
summer sunshine across the bed of the
Anegawa river. By all accounts it was a classic
samurai battle, with much hand-to-hand
fighting with swords. Over the next three
years all other traces of the Asai and Asakura
were eliminated when Nobunaga captured
their castles of Odani and Ichijo ga tani.

## Nobunaga's war against the monks

The militant Buddhists proved far more
intractable to Oda Nobunaga's plans than
any rival *daimyo*. From the early Sengoku
Period these armies, largely recruited from
peasants, had become something of a third
force in Japanese politics. On one occasion
they had even ejected a *daimyo* from his own
province and set up a monk-controlled
territory. The most important grouping from
Oda Nobunaga's point of view were the
Ikko-ikki, fanatics who belonged to the Jodo
Shinshu sect of Buddhism. They brought
about Japan's longest siege when Nobunaga
was forced to spend 10 years, off and on,
reducing their formidable fortress cathedral
called Ishiyama Honganji. This was a long

and bitter campaign directed against a massive castle complex of the latest style situated within a maze of reed beds and creeks. Supplies were run to them by sea, courtesy of the Mori family, and the Ikko-ikki also had large numbers of arquebuses. Their satellite fortress of Nagashima also held out for years, and was finally reduced when Nobunaga piled up dry brushwood against the outer walls and burned them all to death.

However, Nobunaga's most notorious campaign was his raid on the monks of Mount Hiei in 1571. This was probably the only military action of Nobunaga's career so controversial that even some of his own generals opposed the move, but it happened nonetheless. Nobunaga did it for sound military reasons: the Asai and the Asakura

A battle against warrior monks of the Jodo sect, from a model in Okazaki castle. The militant Buddhist armies were the third force in the struggles of the Sengoku Period.

families were then still undefeated, and when marching to Echizen in 1570 Nobunaga had passed beneath the vast bulk of Mount Hiei and realised how it threatened his lines of communication to the north from Kyoto. The holy mountain of Hiei was not ostensibly a military installation. In relation to Kyoto it lay in the 'Demon Gate' quarter, according to *feng shui*, and protected the capital from evil, so it had been revered for centuries. It was the centre of Tendai Buddhism, but during earlier centuries had visited its own wrath upon Kyoto in the form of armies of warrior monks. In Nobunaga's day these warrior monks had allied themselves with the fanatical Ikko-sect confederates against him, and Mount Hiei was an easy target. So in 1571 the mountain was surrounded by a huge army, and Nobunaga's troops simply advanced up the paths and shot or hacked to death every living thing they met, as a warning to any armies, clerical or lay, that dared oppose him.

The fortified monastery of the Ganshoji on the island of
Nagashima, home of one of the fiercest coteries of
warrior monks of the Ikko-ikki.

## Tokugawa Ieyasu and Takeda Shingen

Oda Nobunaga's most powerful *daimyo* rivals
lay in central Japan, where the Takeda,
Uesugi and Hojo all sought his head. When
Nobunaga's ally Tokugawa Ieyasu moved his
headquarters from Okazaki to Hamamatsu in
1570, it was regarded as a highly provocative
act by the Takeda, because Hamamatsu lies
almost at the mouth of the Tenryugawa, the
river draining the mountains of Kai and
Shinano – Takeda Shingen's territory. This
resulted in a mighty showdown between the
old power of the Takeda horsemen and the
up and coming young *daimyo*.

In the early 1570s Takeda Shingen was at
the height of his powers and the backbone
of his army was still his mounted samurai.
His old enemy Uesugi Kenshin was less of a
threat to him now that they had fought their
fifth and final battle at Kawanakajima in
1564, and Shingen realised how cleverly Oda
Nobunaga had succeeded in capturing Kyoto
where Imagawa had failed. The moment was
not yet opportune for Shingen to supplant
Nobunaga, because he still had no easy
access to the Tokaido road. The Tokugawa
possessions would give him this, so
Tokugawa Ieyasu's new base at Hamamatsu
became Shingen's first objective.

Lurking behind Ieyasu was Oda
Nobunaga, whose destruction of Mount Hiei
had given any *daimyo* a perfect excuse for
making war. As a Buddhist monk Takeda
Shingen was in the forefront of those who
wanted revenge. Shingen had also reached a
new understanding with Hojo Ujimasa, who
had become his son-in-law. This safeguarded
his eastern flank, but in case the Hojo
proved treacherous, he had made a further
secret alliance with the families of Satomi

## The Takeda and the triumph of the Tokugawa 1542–1615

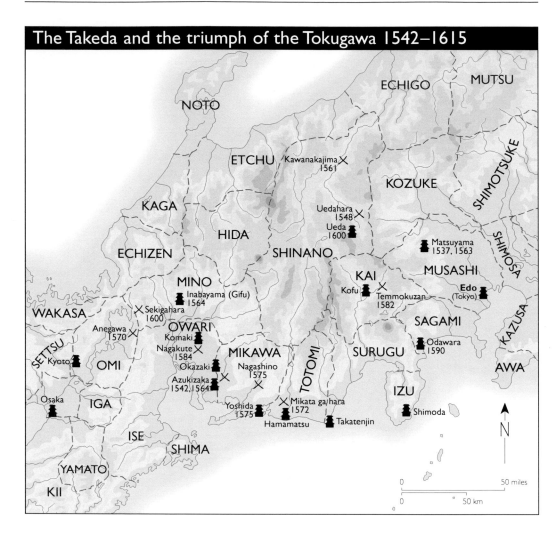

Tokugawa Ieyasu was the third of the great unifiers of Japan. Here we see his successive capitals at Okazaki, Hamamatsu and Edo (Tokyo). His greatest enemy was Takeda Shingen, and we see here the location of Shingen's earlier battles of Ueda and Kawanakajima, and his contest with the Tokugawa at Mikata ga Hara. Ieyasu's subsequent progress included the Komaki campaign and the battle of Sekigahara.

and Satake so that they could descend on Takeda Shingen's rear. One result of the new Takeda/Hojo alliance was that Imagawa Ujizane, the son of the late Imagawa Yoshimoto, was banished from the Hojo domain and went to seek refuge with the man who had once abandoned him – Tokugawa Ieyasu. Nobunaga, meanwhile, was actively courting Uesugi Kenshin, hoping thereby to neutralise any rising by

the Ikko-ikki. Such were the complicated alliances of the Sengoku Period!

When the threat to Hamamatsu became apparent, Nobunaga advised Ieyasu to withdraw to Okazaki and avoid any conflict with Shingen while the building of alliances continued. Ieyasu would have none of it. He was 29 years old and an experienced leader of samurai. Retreat, any retreat, was out of the question, so he stayed defiantly in Hamamatsu, and Takeda Shingen made the first move against him.

Shingen marched his army out of his capital of Kofu in October 1572, relying on the coming snows, rather than the Ikko-ikki, to keep Uesugi Kenshin off his tail. Shingen's first objective in Tokugawa lands was the castle of Futamata. Its capture was entrusted to his son and heir Takeda Katsuyori, who is unfortunately known to history because of his defeat at Nagashino in 1575, but at Futamata he displayed his military talents with some style. Katsuyori had observed that the garrison of Futamata, which was built on the edge of a cliff over the Tenryugawa, collected their water supply from the river by lowering buckets from a rather elaborate wooden water tower. Katsuyori conceived the clever idea of floating heavy wooden rafts down the river to strike against the water tower's supports. The tower eventually collapsed and the garrison surrendered.

## The battle in the snow

Ieyasu was in extreme peril. He had been joined in Hamamatsu by reinforcements from Nobunaga, all of whom were in favour of not attacking Shingen. They reasoned that Shingen's objective was not Ieyasu, but Nobunaga himself, and that Hamamatsu should prepare for a siege. If Shingen's army moved on, leaving a masking force, then perhaps the siege could be broken and Shingen taken in the rear. Ieyasu was still determined to stop Shingen by battle rather than a siege, and it had been reported to him that the Takeda army was drawn up on the high ground of Mikata ga Hara in full battle order. The sight of such a host at close hand encouraged Ieyasu's commanders to try once more to persuade him to withdraw and let the Takeda march past into Mikawa; they could conveniently fall upon the Takeda rear later. Once again Ieyasu dismissed the suggestion, and at about four o'clock in the afternoon, as the snow was beginning to fall, the front ranks of the Tokugawa opened fire on the Takeda samurai.

One curious feature of the battle of Mikata ga Hara that appears in the chronicles is that the Tokugawa opened fire not with bullets or arrows but with stones. Apparently Ieyasu sent a group of peasant soldiers forward into the gathering gloom to intimidate the Takeda into attacking him by throwing stones into their ranks. It had the desired effect, and the Takeda forward troops attacked with great vigour, pushing the stone throwers to one side as they headed forward against the Tokugawa samurai. The Mikawa men withstood the assault well, but the three commanders sent by Nobunaga had not the same spirit for a desperate fight.

At this point the power of the renowned Takeda cavalry came into its own. They were not charging a defensive line as they would do at Nagashino three years later. Instead they were advancing against disordered troops. It was the situation for which the 'horsemen of Kai' had been waiting, and they were led forward across the frozen ground by Takeda Katsuyori, who proved himself to be a fine cavalry leader. It was now getting dark, and seeing the Tokugawa troops reeling, Shingen ordered a general assault by the main body. The charge by the mounted Takeda samurai had proved its worth, and very soon the Tokugawa army was in full retreat.

To put heart into the defenders of Hamamatsu castle Ieyasu had earlier sent to the castle a samurai who had cut the head from a warrior wearing a monk's cowl. He had proclaimed it the head of Shingen, but it had given them only a temporary respite from worry, and the rapid arrival of Ieyasu with apparently only five remaining men made it appear that defeat was certain. Torii Mototada was just giving orders for the gates to be shut and barred when Ieyasu interrupted him. To shut the gates was precisely what Takeda Shingen expected them to do, he reasoned. Instead he ordered for the gates to be left open for their retreating comrades, and huge braziers to be lit to guide them home. To add to this confident air Sakai Tadatsugu took a large war drum and beat it in the tower beside the gate. His lord, apparently well satisfied with the precautions they had taken, took a meal of three bowls of rice and went to sleep. The *Mikawa Fudo-ki* adds that his snores resounded through the room.

As Ieyasu had predicted, when the Takeda advanced to the castle and saw the open gates and the light and heard the drum, they immediately suspected a trick. The *Mikawa Fudo-ki* also has them comment

upon the Tokugawa dead, that all who had
died in the advance lay face downwards,
while those killed in the retreat lay on
their backs. None had turned their backs to
the enemy. The Tokugawa samurai were
men to be reckoned with, so no night-time
assault was made on the castle, and what
'siege lines' there may have been were just
the bivouacs of the Takeda army, who
camped for the night on the battlefield
near Saigadake.

The weather conditions indicated that it
would be an uncomfortable stay, so the
Tokugawa men resolved to make it as
unpleasant as possible, thereby keeping up
the fiction of a strongly defended castle.
It was an area the Tokugawa men knew
well, so they gathered a volunteer force of
16 arquebusiers and 100 other footsoldiers
and attacked the Takeda encampment at
Saigadake, where the plain of Mikata ga Hara
is split by a narrow canyon. The Tokugawa

The battle of Mikata ga Hara in 1572. It was fought in the snow and is famous for a classic cavalry charge by the mounted samurai of the Takeda.

them and cut them as they lay helpless. After the battle, according to legend, local people were troubled by the moans from the ghosts coming from this valley, so in 1574 Ieyasu established a temple at Saigadake called the Soen-do, where a monk called Soen prayed for the repose of the souls. In recent years, when the stream that runs through Saigadake was being culverted, bodies were found in the ground.

The battle of Mikata ga Hara was the first major encounter for Tokugawa Ieyasu, who showed himself to be as much master of psychological warfare as he was a field commander of repute. All the signs now pointed towards a long and desperate siege, and the snows were just beginning. If only they had known the truth about how weakly Hamamatsu was actually defended! In the event Takeda Shingen held a council of war and resolved to withdraw to his mountains and return the following year rather than risk a winter siege of Hamamatsu, which an all-out assault may well have taken. The whole Takeda army pulled back, completely fooled by the Tokugawa.

## The end of the Takeda

Takeda Shingen renewed his attempts to destroy Ieyasu the following year when the snows melted. He returned in early spring of 1573 and chose a different attack route, laying siege to Ieyasu's castle of Noda, on the Toyokawa, in Mikawa province. According to an enduring legend, the defenders, knowing their end was near, decided to dispose of their stocks of sake in the most appropriate manner. The noise of their celebrations could be heard by the besieging camp, who also took note of one samurai who was playing a flute. Takeda Shingen approached the ramparts to hear the tune, and a vigilant guard, who was less drunk than his companions, took an arquebus and put a bullet through the great *daimyo*'s head.

troops led the Takeda back to this ravine, which is about a mile long, 50 yards wide and 100 feet deep in places. Okubo Tadayo is further credited with building a dummy bridge, covered with cloth, across the gap, which seems unlikely as the whole action was fought during one night, though the area round here is still called *Nuno no hashi* ('cloth bridge'). Bridge or not, many scores of Takeda samurai and horses fell into this ravine, where the Tokugawa troops fired on

LEFT Following his defeat at Mikata ga Hara, Tokugawa Ieyasu withdrew to Hamamatsu castle. Sakai Takatsugu beat the war drum in the castle tower to guide their samurai home and confuse the enemy.

BELOW Mori Motonari, whose revenge for the death of his master, Ouchi Yoshitaka, eventually led to the Mori inheriting his domains. The Mori then went on to oppose Oda Nobunaga.

The death of their beloved leader was kept secret for as long as the Takeda could manage. It was the beginning of a long process of rebuilding for the Takeda family, which would eventually be resolved on the field of Nagashino. Here Takeda Katsuyori tried to reproduce the cavalry victory of Mikata ga Hara, but with disastrous results.

Instead of charging disorganised infantry, he led them against disciplined troops behind field fortifications. Almost all the senior commanders of the Takeda were lost in this famous battle, yet the Takeda staggered on for another seven years before being overcome by Tokugawa Ieyasu's troops in 1582.

During the intervening period Tokugawa Ieyasu's ally, Oda Nobunaga, went from strength to the strength. The Mori family were frustrated in their attempts to aid his enemies at the sea battle of Kizugawaguchi in 1578 where they were defeated. There were many more campaigns against the Ikko-ikki at Nagashima and Osaka, where Nobunaga won his final victory against them at Ishiyama Honganji in 1580. In 1576 Nobunaga built Azuchi castle, which became his main base, and conducted campaigns against Ise and Iga provinces in 1580 and 1581. Azuchi was sufficiently far from Kyoto to avoid the periodic uprisings and protests that had always spoiled life in the capital, but it was near enough to allow Nobunaga to control any situation that might arise. So with this magnificent fortress palace to rule from, and numerous loyal allies and generals to serve him, the process of fusion under Oda Nobunaga was well under way.

## Part III: Unification

By 1582 Oda Nobunaga controlled most of central Japan, including Kyoto and the strategic Tokaido and Nakasendo roads to the east. Ishiyama Honganji, the fortified cathedral of the Ikko-ikki, had been taken in 1580, after which triumph Nobunaga had begun to extend his influence westwards for the first time. Two of his most skilled and experienced generals thus began separate but parallel campaigns in this direction. Toyotomi Hideyoshi (who was then called Hashiba Hideyoshi) started the pacification of the southern coast of western Honshu on

the Inland Sea, while his comrade in arms, Akechi Mitsuhide, pursued similar goals on the northern edge of the Sea of Japan.

### The rise of Toyotomi Hideyoshi

Much of Hideyoshi's campaigning was carried out against the Mori family, and the summer of 1582 was to find Hideyoshi sitting patiently in front of Mori's castle of Takamatsu, which a dyked and diverted river

Toyotomi Hideyoshi leaves home to become a samurai, from a painted scroll in the Hokoji temple in Kyoto.

was slowly but very surely flooding. It was at this point in his career that Hideyoshi received the message that was to change his life and with it the destiny of Japan.

The defiance of the Mori had forced Hideyoshi to request reinforcements from Oda Nobunaga, who had hurried to send them on ahead, under Akechi Mitsuhide, intending to follow shortly afterwards himself. This left Nobunaga perilously unguarded, and that night Akechi's army wheeled round and marched back into Kyoto to attack Nobunaga in the Honnoji temple where he was staying. The temple was set on fire and, overwhelmed by superior numbers, Oda Nobunaga committed suicide and his body was consumed in the flames.

Akechi Mitsuhide had done the impossible. He had overcome the most powerful man in Japan. Somewhat stunned

The walls of Tottori castle, which is built into the wooded hillside. Tottori was the site of the tragic starvation campaign of 1581, where the defenders are alleged to have resorted to cannibalism.

by his own success, he immediately proclaimed himself shogun and ordered the extermination of Nobunaga's five sons. Only Toyotomi Hideyoshi now had the military capacity to react swiftly to this astounding development. Keeping the awful news secret, he hastily patched together a surrender agreement with Mori and force-marched his army back to Kyoto to avenge his dead master, an act that would not only bestow upon him an enormous moral superiority over the treacherous Akechi Mitsuhide, but would also be likely to provide undreamed of material and political gain.

Very soon the new shogun received the news that a hostile army was on its way to destroy him. Having been taken completely by surprise at Hideyoshi's quick reactions, Mitsuhide marched downstream along the Yodo river and took up a position against his rival's advance behind a small river

commanded by a hill near the village of Yamazaki. Beginning with a completely successful storming of the wooded hill, Hideyoshi trounced Mitsuhide, whose men fled in all directions, and the fugitive shogun of 13 days was eventually murdered by a peasant gang.

## The Shizugatake campaign

Hideyoshi won the battle of Yamazaki in the name of the late Oda Nobunaga, not in the name of his surviving sons, who, as Akechi had already realised, were the main hindrance against anyone else benefiting personally from Nobunaga's death. Most inconveniently for Hideyoshi's future plans, Akechi's brief coup had only resulted in the deaths of two of them: the youngest, killed alongside his father at the Honnoji, and the eldest, his heir Nobutada, who was killed later at Nijo castle.

This print shows Hideyoshi's political masterstroke, which was to sponsor the cause of the infant Samboshi, the grandson of the late Oda Nobunaga, at the expense of Nobunaga's two surviving brothers.

Toyotomi Hideyoshi, the second of the great unifiers, as depicted in a waxwork at the Ise Sengoku Village.

The victorious and magnanimous Hideyoshi then generously adopted the fourth son Hidekatsu, who was barely 15 years old, leaving just two adult sons, Nobuo and Nobutaka, to provide any opposition. In a diplomatic masterstroke Hideyoshi played upon the obvious rivalry between the two surviving brothers and forced them to agree that, by the simple principle of primogeniture, the late Nobutada's infant son Samboshi, Oda Nobunaga's grandson by his declared heir, should be declared the new inheritor of the Oda domain. At the same time Hideyoshi tried to make it appear that out of the two regents, he favoured Oda Nobuo above Nobutaka. The result was that Nobunaga's other generals, who had fought shoulder to shoulder with Hideyoshi for many years, were forced to declare for one regent or the other, thus splitting any potential opposition to the takeover that Hideyoshi was really planning for himself.

Had Hideyoshi's fellow generals and the two regents cooperated against him, then the chance of a Toyotomi triumph would have been very slim, because between them they had Hideyoshi surrounded. Oda Nobuo was based in his late father's castle of Kiyosu, which sat squarely on the Tokaido to the east, while Nobutaka dominated the Nakasendo to the north-east from mighty Gifu. Further north still was a loose coalition of former Oda generals under the overall leadership of Shibata Katsuie, who could march on Kyoto from Echizen province; another general, Takigawa Kazumasu, was located near to Nobuo, at the fortress of Kameyama on the Pacific coast. Fortunately for Hideyoshi, his rivals came dramatically to his assistance early in 1583, when Oda Nobutaka foolishly decided to attack Hideyoshi before the snow had melted in the Echizen mountain passes. This meant that his ally Shibata Katsuie could not move to help him. Fully appreciating this point, Hideyoshi moved rapidly against Gifu, and such was his reputation for successful siegework that Nobutaka immediately surrendered.

On arriving back in Kyoto, Hideyoshi learned that Takigawa Kazumasu in Kameyama had also revolted and was planning a two-pronged attack in conjunction with Shibata Katsuie's son Katsutoyo. The latter was based in Nagahama castle, on the eastern shore of Lake Biwa, and was unaffected by the winter weather. Hideyoshi first marched to Nagahama and bought its surrender with a large bribe, then,

with his rear secure, and the hapless Oda Nobuo still thinking that Hideyoshi was doing all this on his behalf, Hideyoshi turned on Kameyama and conducted the first successful siege of a Japanese castle involving the use of mines to collapse a section of wall.

Spring was now on its way, and the thaw would free Shibata Katsuie from his frozen fastness. To guard against this, Hideyoshi sent several detachments of troops north of Lake Biwa to strengthen the existing garrisons of the mountain-top forts that covered the Hokkokukaido. When spring came and the snow in the Echizen passes melted away, Shibata Katsuie led his army south, and just as Hideyoshi had expected, his yamashiro provided a genuine barrier, so Katsuie set up his positions on other mountains opposite. The two front lines were now separated by just under two miles, with the mountain peak of Tenjin and its adjacent valleys acting as a no-man's land between them. The northern army totalled about 20,000 men.

Hideyoshi then marched north to join his frontier force, but no sooner did he arrive at Kinomoto, the nearest town to the fortress line, than he had to leave to face a serious threat to his rear. Having heard of the developments, Oda Nobutaka in Gifu, whom Hideyoshi had generously allowed to retain possession both of the castle and his own head, regretted his earlier surrender and threw his weight behind the northern army that had come to his aid. Hideyoshi was therefore forced to march back and along the Nakasendo with 20,000 men to besiege Gifu once again, but he wisely based himself in the nearby fortress on Ogaki, which lay on the same road, just in case Shibata Katsuie should break through in the north. Hideyoshi left on 17 April and started the attack on Gifu early on 19 April.

## The battle on the mountain-tops
Shortly after Hideyoshi's departure, Katsuie's vanguard began the serious business of capturing the frontier forts. The tactics he chose were very clever: he first concentrated

Takayama Ukon, one of the best-known Christian *daimyo*, shown here on a devotional picture from Osaka.

on the forts to the west of the road, where the garrisons were weakest. With Maeda Toshiie providing a rearguard, and masking the minor outposts to their left, the assaults concentrated first on Oiwa and then on Iwasaki by circling round to the west of Lake Yogo. This allowed Katsuie's men to advance against them from the south-west, along the mountain ridge, rather than by a frontal assault from the more difficult northern side, while the garrison at Shizugatake would not dare sally out to challenge them. The men across the valley were now perilously isolated, and they were to be the next target. This attack would be led by Shibata Katsuie's main body. Then, with all the peaks secured, Hideyoshi's rearguard, under Hashiba Hidenaga, could be wiped out and the mountain pass would be secure.

At first all went well for Sakuma Morimasa, who led the initial advance. Oiwa was first to fall, and its commander, Nakagawa Kiyohide, was killed. Iwasaki fell soon afterwards, following an attack along the ridge from the south, but its commander, Takayama Ukon, escaped across the Hokkokukaido to Tagami. Apart from the two smaller forward positions, Sakuma Morimasa now occupied all of Hideyoshi's castles west of the road except for Shizugatake, upon which he could now concentrate all his forces. Having watched his two comrades along the ridge lose their castles, Kuwayama Shigeharu and his 1,000 men in Shizugatake must have been

very apprehensive about their fate. Yet it does not seem to have diminished their fighting spirit; nor was there any question of surrender.

On the other side, Shibata Katsuie became more concerned with every hour that passed about how dangerously vulnerable Sakuma Morimasa was to a counter-attack. Hashiba Hidenaga, after all, was just across the valley with 15,000 men, and Katsuie also knew that another of Hideyoshi's allies, Niwa Nagahide, was not too far away, on Lake Biwa with 2,000 men. There was also the question of Toyotomi Hideyoshi, but by all accounts he and his 20,000 strong army were every bit as engrossed with the siege of Gifu as Sakuma Morimasa was with the siege of Shizugatake. Nevertheless, the prudent Katsuie sent a messenger to Morimasa ordering him to abandon his open siege lines for the security of newly captured Oiwa. Morimasa rejected the idea. Shizugatake would be his before night fell, and he dismissed out of hand any

The samurai Niwa Nagahide in action at the decisive battle of Yamazaki in 1582, which destroyed the usurper Akechi Mitsuhide.

suggestion that Hideyoshi could return to its relief when he was entangled with Gifu. So Morimasa disobeyed the orders of his commanding officer and stayed fighting, while from Shizugatake, Kuwayama battled on, refusing to let Morimasa win a hat-trick. Six times Shibata Katsuie sent the order, and six times Morimasa refused to comply.

By now a messenger had galloped the 32 miles to Ogaki with the intelligence for Hideyoshi that Oiwa and Iwasaki had fallen, and that Shizugatake was likely to follow. When asked if Morimasa had withdrawn into Oiwa, the messenger replied that he had not. At this moment, according to the chronicler of

*Hideyoshi's army in the field. Toyotomi Hideyoshi grew to command the largest armies ever deployed in Japan.*

the battle, Hideyoshi's expression changed from sorrow to one of glee. 'Then I have won!' he is said to have exclaimed. His long military experience had told him that Sakuma Morimasa had gone a ridge too far.

Very early in the morning of 20 April Hideyoshi made ready to rush back to Kinomoto. He left 5,000 men to continue the siege of Gifu and began a great gamble. The only way he could achieve surprise was by taking an entirely mounted army with him while the infantry and supplies marched along far behind. It was an enormous risk to separate the different units of his army in this way, but it was a chance that Hideyoshi had to take.

Burning pine torches lit the way as Hideyoshi's army of 1,000 mounted samurai

hurried along the familiar and well trodden road. A main body of 15,000 men brought up the rear, but the gap between the two lengthened by the second. From Ogaki the ride took them through Sekigahara, a village whose name was to become very familiar 20 years later, and on to Kinomoto, which they reached just five hours after leaving Ogaki. The first that Sakuma Morimasa knew of their arrival was the sudden appearance of 1,000 burning pine torches down in the valley. Hideyoshi paused only to collect Hashiba Hidenaga's troops in Tagami and to be apprised of the situation. Then, following a signal from a conch shell trumpet blown, it is said, by Hideyoshi himself, his eager and impatient men poured up the mountain paths towards Shizugatake and Sakuma's siege lines.

Battles fought on the tops of mountains are not a common occurrence in military history. Even in a country like Japan, where mountains are plentiful and many have castles or the remains of them on their summits, mountain-top conflicts either tended to be sieges, or consisted of actions fought in the valleys below with the hill-tops being used solely as vantage points. This is what makes Shizugatake almost unique. It was not a siege, but a field engagement, except that the 'field' lay on the tops and along the ridges of a wooded mountain chain. It was also fought as the result of a surprise attack by night on an unsuspecting enemy. The twist here is that the army which was both surprised and defeated was the one that up until that point had been holding the high ground!

The first armed contact was made as dawn was breaking. All along the mountain paths and in among the trees numerous small group and individual combats took place. There were no lines of well-drilled arquebusiers as at Nagashino. Instead a huge disjointed melee began, with Hideyoshi's mounted vanguard playing a leading role. Spears, swords and daggers decided the outcome of Shizugatake, not blocks of pikemen, and the heroes of the hour were the seven valiant warriors named as the 'Seven Spears of Shizugatake', who were all members of Hideyoshi's own mounted bodyguard.

As the first of Sakuma Morimasa's retreating troops came hurtling down into the valley or along the further ridges towards Katsuie's headquarters, Shibata Katsuie realised that the day was lost. Hoping to save as many of his army as he could, he ordered a general retreat, and made it safely back to Kitanosho castle with Hideyoshi in hot pursuit. In order to complete the business, Toyotomi Hideyoshi continued north and laid siege to Kitanosho. All that Katsuie had to defend the place were 3,000 survivors of Shizugatake. As the third and second baileys fell, he retired to the keep with the members of his family and resolved to go to his death in spectacular samurai fashion. The keep was

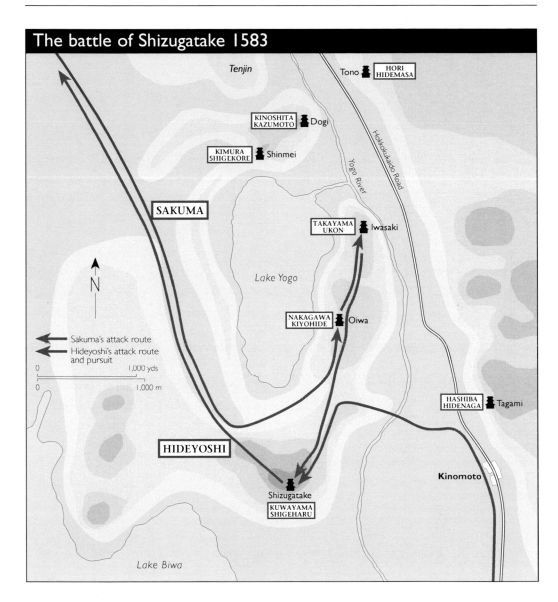

## The battle of Shizugatake 1583

Tenjin

Tono  HORI HIDEMASA

KINOSHITA KAZUMOTO  Dogi

KIMURA SHIGEKORE  Shinmei

SAKUMA

TAKAYAMA UKON  Iwasaki

Lake Yogo

Yogo River

Hokkokaido Road

N

Sakuma's attack route
Hideyoshi's attack route
and pursuit

0            1,000 yds
0            1,000 m

NAKAGAWA KIYOHIDE  Oiwa

HASHIBA HIDENAGA  Tagami

HIDEYOSHI

Kinomoto

Shizugatake
KUWAYAMA SHIGEHARU

Lake Biwa

ABOVE This map shows the stages of the battle of Shizugatake. Sakuma Morimasa attacked Shizugatake fort after capturing the other castles on the ridge. Hideyoshi then came galloping to its relief.

LEFT Shibata Katsuie, whose army was defeated at Shizugatake, as depicted on his statue on the site of Kitanosho castle in Fukui.

filled with loose straw which was set on fire, and Shibata Katsuie committed *hara kiri* among the flames. Today, all that is left of Kitanosho castle is a fragment of wall consisting of a few stones beside a main road in Fukui. On top sits a memorial to Fukui's

most famous son, in the shape of a fierce-looking statue of Shibata Katsuie, personally undefeated, but betrayed by a subordinate who would not obey orders and so suffered one of the most unusual defeats in samurai history.

## The Komaki campaign

The only foe who now opposed Hideyoshi in the immediate vicinity of his territories was Tokugawa Ieyasu. They met at the battle of Nagakute in 1584, a remarkable but indecisive fight which took place largely as a result of boredom! The two sides had each

The site of the battle of Shizugatake in 1583. This unusual contest was a field battle fought along a mountain ridge. With his victory at Shizugatake, Toyotomi Hideyoshi secured his position in central Japan.

built a line of field fortifications near Komaki, which they defended with thousands of arquebuses. The resulting stalemate, brought about because both commanders had experienced the devastating effects of gunfire at Nagashino in 1575, encouraged Hideyoshi to send his troops to raid Tokugawa territory. The Tokugawa followed them, and a field battle was fought miles from either fortification line. Nagakute, although very bloody in its execution, was far from decisive, and both Hideyoshi and Ieyasu soon realised that they had little to gain from fighting one another. There followed a ritual exchange of hostages to cement the agreement.

## The war for the islands

With his rear secure, Toyotomi Hideyoshi then turned his attentions towards Japan's other two main islands of Shikoku and Kyushu. The campaign for the former was brief: Chosokabe's part-time army was no match for Hideyoshi's professionals. The Chosokabe men, who were renowned for being so ready to serve that they tilled the fields with their spears thrust into the paths between the rice paddies, were soon swept aside, and Chosokabe Motochika paid homage. The invasion of Kyushu was a different matter altogether, and to understand why it is necessary to backtrack a few years to see how Kyushu's own brand of Sengoku *daimyo* had established a world of their own in southern Japan.

When the Ryuzoji were defeated at Okita Nawate in 1584, little stood in the way of a Shimazu conquest of the whole of Kyushu island. The Otomo were the one major *daimyo* family left, and the Shimazu were bearing down upon them when a dramatic new factor entered the equation. Just as little Arima had asked for help from mighty Shimazu in 1584, so did the mighty Otomo ask for help in 1586 from the 'super-mighty' Toyotomi Hideyoshi.

The result was the biggest military operation ever seen in Japan, involving the transportation of huge armies across the straits from Shikoku and Honshu. Two separate armies marched down opposite sides of Kyushu, defeating Shimazu forces as they went and gaining allies by the score. On the west coast the island lords such as Goto and Matsuura hurried to pledge allegiance to Hideyoshi, and the forces

converged on the Shimazu capital of Kagoshima. A battle was fought at the Sendai river, and then all that was left were the volcanic gullies that protected the last Shimazu outpost. There could have been the greatest act of mass suicide in samurai history, but instead a negotiated settlement was agreed, and the noble and ancient Shimazu family submitted to the upstart Hideyoshi.

Following the defeat of the Shimazu the territorial map was redrawn, and several of Hideyoshi's loyal generals, such as Kato Kiyomasa, found themselves becoming Kyushu landlords. These were the men that formed the core of Hideyoshi army for the invasion of Korea in 1592, a major expedition that will be told through the life of a participant, Kato Kiyomasa.

## The island of Kyushu during the Sengoku Period

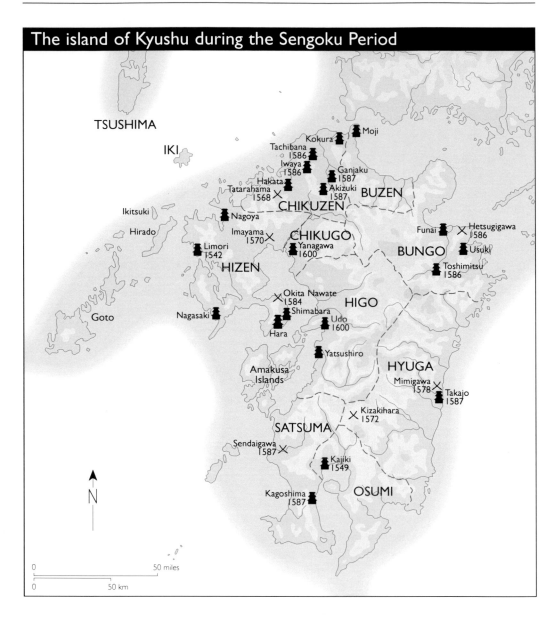

Until 1587 the southern island of Kyushu existed in a world of its own. This map shows the struggles between the Otomo, Ryuzoji, Arima and Shimazu families, and the dramatic invasion by Toyotomi Hideyoshi in 1587.

Only the far north of Japan now remained unconquered. The story of the defeat of the last of the Hojo at Odawara has already been told, and once they fell, the remaining northern lords surrendered almost without a shot being fired. By 1591 the process of fusion, the reunification of Japan, was complete. For Japan, at least, the Age of Warring States appeared to be over.

# Kato Kiyomasa (1562–1611)

One of the most striking features of the Sengoku Period was the way the turbulence and disorder of the age allowed men from relatively obscure backgrounds to achieve great power and influence through the exercise of their military skills. Every foot soldier, it seemed, carried a general's war fan in his knapsack. The greatest example of such a rise to power was, of course, Toyotomi Hideyoshi, who made sure that no one else could follow his lead by the Sword Hunt and Separation Edicts of 1587 and 1591, which disarmed the peasants and made a clear distinction between samurai and farmers. Before the ladder of promotion had been removed, however, at least one other commoner from Hideyoshi's home village made his own rise to martial stardom. His name was Kato Kiyomasa.

Born in the village of Nakamura, which has long since been swallowed up within the modern city of Nagoya, Kato Kiyomasa was called Toranosuke (the young tiger) in his childhood. He was the son of a blacksmith who died when the boy was three years old. Toyotomi Hideyoshi was from the same village, and young Toranosuke saw the example he set of leaving the peasant life and enlisting as a soldier in the armies of Oda Nobunaga. Through a familial relationship between the two boys' mothers, Toyotomi Hideyoshi took Toranosuke under his wing when his father died.

Kato Kiyomasa soon proved to have a considerable aptitude for the military life, and his first opportunity to demonstrate it came at the age of 21 in the battle of Shizugatake, where the absence of a flat battlefield and lines of arquebus troops allowed the individual samurai spirit to be

expressed in an unfettered way. Kato Kiyomasa fought from horseback in classic style, with the support of a loyal band of samurai attendants, and wielded his favourite cross-bladed spear to great effect. It was not long before a number of enemy heads had fallen to Kiyomasa, and to intimidate his opponents he had one of his attendants tie the severed heads to a long stalk of green bamboo and carry it into Kato's fresh conflicts like a general's standard. Kato Kiyomasa was named that day as one of the Seven Spears of

Kato Kiyomasa, as depicted in the statue of him outside Kumamoto castle. He is wearing his famous tall helmet.

Shizugatake – the most valiant warriors – and from that time on his fortunes prospered.

In 1585 Kato Kiyomasa received from Hideyoshi the important role of Kazue no kami, effectively Hideyoshi's inspector of taxes, and in 1588 he began a long association with the island of Kyushu through the following sequence of events. A *daimyo* called Sasa Narimasa had sided against Hideyoshi at the time of the Komaki campaign of 1584, but had been defeated and forced to submit to Hideyoshi's rule. Following the Kyushu campaign in 1587, Sasa was transferred to captured territory in northern Higo province, but Hideyoshi was so dissatisfied with his behaviour that Sasa was forced to commit suicide.

Kato Kiyomasa was given Sasa's fief, centred around the castle town of Kumamoto, where he was to be based for the rest of his life, and the city still honours the memory of its most famous inhabitant. Statues of Kiyomasa abound, and all show him in full armour with a striking helmet design. It was supposed to represent a courtier's cap, and was made by building up a crown of wood and papier-mâché on top of a simple helmet bowl. Several of these helmets still exist. Two, which are lacquered black, may be seen in Kumamoto, while a silver one with a red rising sun on each side is preserved in Nagoya. Some portraits of Kiyomasa also show him with an extensive beard, which was quite unusual for a samurai.

Another characteristic of Kiyomasa was his fanatical attachment to the Nichiren sect of Buddhism, to the extent of using a saying of Nichiren – *Namu myoho renge kyo* (Hail to the Lotus of the Divine Law) – as his motto and war cry. It was also inscribed on the breastplates of his foot soldiers, and his most treasured possession was a white flag with the same motto, said to have been written by Nichiren himself. This was carried as his battle standard in every encounter he fought. Kato's religious affiliation contrasted markedly with the Christianity espoused by his neighbour in southern Higo, Konishi Yukinaga, and the two men did not enjoy friendly relations.

In 1592 the invasion of Korea was launched, and Kato Kiyomasa was given command of the Second Division of the Japanese army. Unfortunately his rival, Konishi Yukinaga, was given command of the First Division. So easy was Konishi's landing and so rapid was his progress up Korea that it seemed that there would be little glory left for Kato Kiyomasa's troops. In fact, by the time the Second Division caught up with the First at Ch'ungju, Konishi's men had reaped all the battle honours. A furious row then broke out between the two commanders over who should now lead the final advance on Seoul. A compromise was reached by which the two divisions took separate routes, but again Konishi beat his rival to the glory of being first into battle, because when Kato Kiyomasa arrived at the gates of the capital he found Konishi's men on guard duty, and he had to persuade them to let him in!

Konishi's troops were tired after their 20-day march through Korea, so it was sensibly agreed that Kato's division should now take the lead and pursue the retreating Koreans northwards. Kato Kiyomasa set off in high spirits, only to come to a grinding halt on the southern bank of the wide Imjin river. There he sat for almost a month, and it was only when an unwise Korean raid presented the Japanese with some boats that a crossing was made. By this time the king of Korea had made his escape, and at a council of war held in Seoul, the Japanese high command agreed that Konishi should continue northwards in pursuit of the king, while Kato Kiyomasa headed north-east after the two Korean princes who had taken refuge somewhere near the Tumen river.

Kato Kiyomasa's campaign in Hamgyong province, the wildest area of Korea, was the crowning glory of his military career. He crossed the peninsula from Seoul and made his way along the east coast, meeting his first armed resistance at the battle of Songjin, where a Korean army trapped Kiyomasa's force inside a rice warehouse. The Japanese defended the position so well, with massed arquebus fire from behind barricades of rice bales, that the Korean general withdrew for the night. Without waiting for the next day Kato launched a night raid, and drove the Korean soldiers into a trap. As the Korean general then fled north, creating panic as he went, Kato's subsequent progress was made that much easier.

He eventually caught up with the Korean princes at Hoeryong, a Korean penal colony on the Tumen, where he discovered to his surprise and delight that the princes had been taken captive by their own rebellious subjects. With his primary objective attained, Kato Kiyomasa resolved to invade China, or at least a few square miles of it immediately across the border. Here lived the Jurchens, called the Orangai by the Japanese, and with Koreans acting as guides, Kato Kiyomasa became the first, and only, Japanese general to enter China during the Korean campaign. The Jurchens proved to be stubborn fighters, and at one stage Kiyomasa had to take his precious Nichiren flag in his own hands when his standard bearer was killed. Following this excursion, the Second Division followed the Tumen down to the sea, and enjoyed a moment of poetic whimsy on the beach at

Sosup'o, where an offshore island looked like Mount Fuji.

It was about this time that developments elsewhere in Korea sounded the death knell for the Japanese invasion, and within a few months Kato Kiyomasa was to be found first defending his line of forts and then abandoning them altogether as the army regrouped at Seoul. A retreat to the coast followed, where Kato Kiyomasa took a prominent part in the last siege of the first invasion at Chinju, and he is credited with the use of reinforced wooden wagons to protect footsoldiers digging away the foundation stones of the wall to create a breach.

Kato's troops garrisoned the fort of Sosaengp'o as his contribution to the limited occupation of Korean territory that was carried out by Japan over the next four years. Tiger hunting was a popular relief from boredom, and many prints and paintings depict Kato Kiyomasa in this role. Tiger meat was shipped back to Japan in the hope that it would restore Hideyoshi's failing health, and on one occasion a live tiger was taken

Kato Kiyomasa in a more peaceful vein, shown in the tea room built into the outer defences of Kumamoto castle.

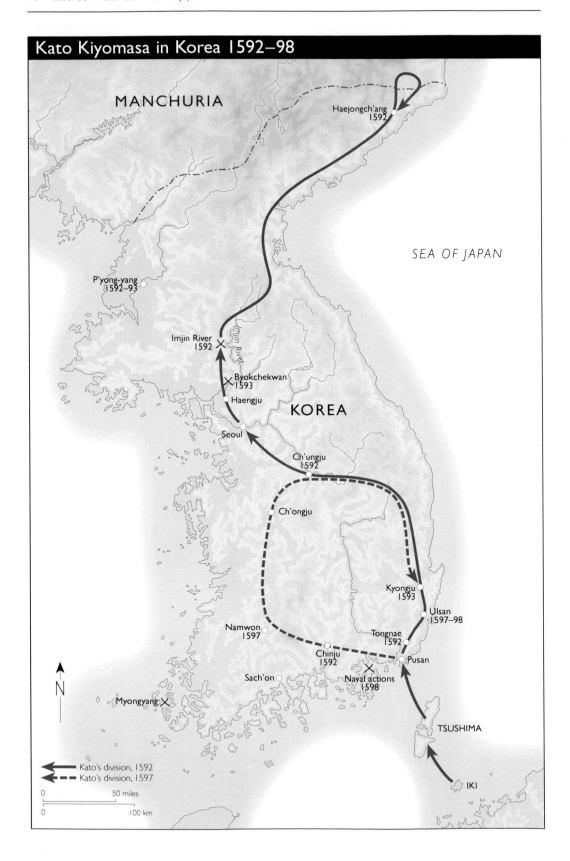

## Kato Kiyomasa in Korea 1592–98

MANCHURIA

Haejongch'ang
1592

SEA OF JAPAN

P'yong-yang
(1592–93)

Imjin River
1592

Imjin River

Byokchekwan
1593

Haengju

KOREA

Seoul

Ch'ungju
1592

Ch'ongju

Kyongju
1593

Ulsan
1597–98

Namwon
1597

Tongnae
1592

Chinju
1592

Pusan

Sach'on

Naval actions
1598

Myongyang

TSUSHIMA

IKI

N

Kato's division, 1592
Kato's division, 1597

0          50 miles
0              100 km

into an assembly of the great *daimyo*. It caused alarm when it pulled away from the keepers who were holding it back with chains, and approached Kato Kiyomasa, who fixed it with such a fierce glare that the tiger is said to have stopped dead in its tracks!

Kato Kiyomasa was one of the leading generals put into the field when the Japanese invaded Korea for a second time in 1597. He took part in the capture of Hwangsoksan castle, but his most important role was in defence of the fortress of Ulsan during a long and bitter winter siege, when soldiers froze to death at their posts. Kiyomasa had come to Ulsan from Sosaengp'o, with a small force, and he immediately took charge of the situation, inspiring his men to hold out until a relieving army arrived, in spite of 'human wave' attacks against the walls by thousands of Chinese.

LEFT The route of Kato's division is shown for the 1592 and 1597 invasions, together with his campaign into Manchuria and his defence of Ulsan

BELOW The siege of Ulsan castle during the winter of 1597/8, one of the most bitter campaigns of the Korean War.

On his return to Japan, Kato Kiyomasa took over his manorial responsibilities at Kumamoto once again, and because of the unpleasant experience of being besieged in Ulsan, he resolved to make Kumamoto castle impregnable. He planted nut trees within the baileys to provide food, and all the mats within the living quarters were stuffed not with the usual rice straw but with dried vegetable stalks, so that even they could be eaten in an emergency. It would no doubt have given Kiyomasa great satisfaction if he had known that Kumamoto castle would indeed withstand a siege in 1871!

When the *daimyo* split into the two factions that led to the Sekigahara campaign of 1600, Kiyomasa's remoteness from the scene meant that he could take a more calculated view of the likely outcome than many of his contemporaries. His old rival and neighbour Konishi Yukinaga declared for Ishida Mitsunari and lost his head as a result, so Kiyomasa was quick to seize for himself the other half of Higo province in the name of Tokugawa Ieyasu. Yet there was a less selfish reason for Kato's choice, because Toyotomi Hideyori, Hideyoshi's heir, was still

alive, and Kato's loyalty to Hideyoshi's memory led him to believe that Hideyori would be safer if there was peace between him and the Tokugawa. Hideyori was present at a meeting held in Nijo castle to discuss his future, and it is said that Kiyomasa had a dagger concealed on his person which he intended to use on the shogun if Hideyori's safety was threatened. As it happened, Kato Kiyomasa did not live long enough to witness the death of Hideyori at Osaka castle, because he died himself in 1611, possibly from the effects of poison, and Tokugawa Ieyasu may have had a hand in his death.

Like several other Sengoku *daimyo*, Kato Kiyomasa left writings behind in which he tried to make recommendations for the successful samurai life. His *Precepts* include the following observations:

*One should rise at four in the morning, practise sword techniques, eat one's breakfast and train with the bow, the gun and the horse.*

*If one should require diversions, one should make them such outdoor pastimes as falconry, deer hunting and wrestling.*

*The practice of Noh [style] dancing is absolutely forbidden. When one unsheathes one's sword, one has the cutting down of people in mind. As all things are born from what lies in the heart, a samurai who practises dancing, which lies outside the martial arts, should be ordered to commit hara kiri.*

*Having been born into the house of a warrior, one's intentions should be to take hold of a long and a short sword and die. If a man does not explore the nature of bushido everyday, it will be difficult for him to die a brave and manly death.*

# The end of the farmer-warrior

When the process of fusion was nearing its completion, Toyotomi Hideyoshi enacted two laws that were to change the face of Japan as much as had the wars of the Sengoku Period. He first realised that one reason why organisations such as the Ikko-ikki had been able to challenge samurai rule too easily was because of the ready supply of weapons. The resulting Sword Hunt of 1587 was designed to disarm anyone who might oppose Hideyoshi's control. Over a short period Hideyoshi's troops entered villages and confiscated all swords, spears and guns. The process did not stop at the peasantry: minor *daimyo* whose loyalty was questionable, village headmen, temples and shrines were all relieved of their weapons.

The Separation Edict of 1591 enshrined in law the situation that had been developing for at least 20 years. The increased professionalism of armies had meant that untrained peasants given a spear or a gun could be more of a hindrance than a help, so this informal trend towards a separation between the military and agricultural function was made both legal and rigid. No longer could someone like Hideyoshi himself enlist as a foot soldier and be promoted to general. If you were classified as a farmer, then your function in life was to grow food while others did the fighting.

Up till then farmers and samurai had overlapped considerably in their status and functions. There were poor samurai who farmed and fought part-time, and there were rich village headmen who lived the lives of lords of the manor. Yet although the farmers had to contend with poverty, high taxation, typhoons and the occasional famine, in some ways they were much better off than their European contemporaries. Since the wars of the Sengoku Period were civil wars, there is a refreshing absence of peasant

massacres that so often formed part of an invasion of one European country by another in the 16th century. Since any oppressed peasant could easily cross a provincial border to till the fields of an enemy, cruelty against civilians was also not to be recommended. So were the samurai immune from the tendency to random violence and economic devastation inherent in contemporary Europe?

This is a considerable question, and it is quite clear that Takeda Shingen was genuinely popular with all sections of society in the territories he ruled so well. It is also interesting to note that the most dramatic example of a peasant uprising against a cruel *daimyo* occurred two decades after the civil wars had ceased. This was the Shimabara Rebellion of 1637/38, directed against the tyrant Matsukura Shigemasa, who was given to tying peasants up inside straw raincoats and setting fire to them. From this it may be argued that if Matsukura had lived at a time when one's neighbour was by definition one's rival, then self-interest alone would have prevented him from acting in such an outrageous manner. It is when the argument is taken one stage further that credulity is strained. The behaviour of Japanese forces abroad during the 20th century is then seen as an aberration of the samurai tradition, and not in any way as its consequence.

It is indeed difficult to tease out much evidence of deliberate civilian casualties from contemporary Japanese writings, though this may simply be that the compilers did not think that such matters were worth recording. The absence of fortified towns meant that Japanese sieges were conducted against almost purely military installations, where civilian casualties would be few. In fact, when Otsu was besieged in 1600, the local people took their picnic boxes along to a nearby hillside to watch the fun! When Takeda Shingen was repulsed before Odawara castle in 1569, he burned the town of Odawara before retiring, but when Toyotomi Hideyoshi took Kagoshima in 1587 and Odawara in 1590, there was nothing that remotely resembled the sack of a European town. By contrast, civilian deaths are implied in the accounts of wars conducted against peasant armies, such as Nobunaga's campaign against the Ikko-ikki sectarians or the Shimabara Rebellion, where the distinction between soldier and non-combatant was blurred and the rebels took shelter in fortresses along with their families.

Ordinary people could of course get caught up in the fighting through no fault of their own. Sometimes they were drawn to the site of a conflict by thoughts of self-preservation, and the numbers of people within a castle would be swelled by farmers and others moving in for safety when an attack was imminent. This could stretch the garrison's resources and provisions to their limits. When Takeda Shingen invaded the Kanto in 1569 the local people flocked to Odawara, causing severe pressure on resources. During Hideyoshi's invasion of the Hojo territories a much larger move of population took place, and the garrisons of nearly all the Hojo satellite castles were left as skeleton staff while most troops were packed into Odawara. Hojo Ujikuni's Hachigata castle was the sole exception, and came under attack itself. Hideyoshi's support forces under Uesugi Kagekatsu and Maeda Toshiie spread 35,000 troops round Hachigata, and after a month-long siege Ujikuni surrendered, thus providing a foretaste of what was to come at Odawara. Starvation was but one of

the weapons Hideyoshi employed at Odawara, and to drive the point home the besiegers created a town of their own around the walls, where they feasted loudly within sight of the defenders.

However, the Korean campaign added a different dimension. Here the fortified town often replaced the isolated castle as a battle site, and many civilian deaths must be inferred from the huge number of heads taken at such conflicts as Chinju and Namwon. The samurai were now operating in a foreign country far from home, and reports of atrocities are well substantiated. The so-called Ear Mound in Kyoto, where are interred the noses cut off as trophies from the dead in Korea, include the remains of women and children.

In a similar attitude to that shown to the agricultural arm, the wealth of towns and ports may have been coveted by rival *daimyo*, but it was certainly not in their interests to destroy the geese that laid the golden eggs. Artists, architects, sword makers and tea masters were a vital part of a *daimyo*'s world, because the beauty and elegance they gave to a *daimyo*'s life was every bit as important as the need to maintain his military bearing.

Respect for religious institutions was somewhat more hit and miss, and depended upon whether the *daimyo* was affiliated to the Buddhist sect that annoyed him. Nobunaga carried out his notorious massacre at Mount Hiei because it suited his purpose, but after the defeat of the Ikko-ikki, both Hideyoshi and Ieyasu courted the religious authorities who had once spawned the rebels. Funds were made available to rebuild their temples, although with necessary safeguards so that they could not revolt again.

# Sen Rikyu (1522–91)

Of all the civilians who practised their trade on a *daimyo*'s behalf, none exerted greater influence than those who had mastered the art of tea, and it is impossible to understand the minds of the Sengoku *daimyo* without appreciating the central importance in their lives of the Japanese tea ceremony. *Cha no yu*, or *Chado*, the 'way of tea' at the same time a quasi religious ritual, a means of developing group solidarity and the most subtle way of gaining and exercising political influence.

Behind these enthusiasts for tea, which included almost all the *daimyo*, lay the arbiters of how the tea ceremony should be performed. Their influence was enormous, and the most influential of them all was Sen Rikyu, who is sometimes known as Sen Soeki. He was born in 1522, the son of a wholesale fish merchant in the town of Sakai, to the south of Osaka, on the coast of the Inland Sea. His family had no military connections, but it was through exercising influence over military men that the wealthy merchants of Sakai such as Rikyu's father made their mark on Japanese society. Also,

Sen Rikyu, greatest of the tea masters and the confidant of both Oda Nobunaga and Toyotomi Hideyoshi.

The tea house in the garden of the Taizo-In temple in Kyoto, viewed across the ornamental pond.

by organising themselves into a governing body the burghers of Sakai won for their city a certain independence and immunity from the chaos of the Sengoku Period.

Religion and the arts flourished within the safety of Sakai, with local Zen temples being particularly well patronised, and nowhere did Zen and aesthetics come together more harmoniously than through the performance of the tea ceremony.

Ashikaga Yoshimasa, the shogun of the silver temple, had been an early and enthusiastic patron, and many of the traditions associated with tea had come from the exquisite rituals performed by Yoshimasa and his court. The comparatively relaxed atmosphere of wealthy Sakai allowed the tea ceremony to develop beyond Yoshimasa's important early input, and it was there that Sen Rikyu became a tea master.

Unlike the comparative flamboyance of Yoshimasa's parties at the Ginkakuji, Sen Rikyu took the Zen principles of simplicity and economy as his model. His tea house was a thatched hut, and from this unostentatious beginning the tea ceremony flowered into a ritual centred around the sharing of a bowl of tea in a manner characterised by restraint. This principle extended to design of the rough and simple pottery used as tea vessels, but it was not long before the canny merchants of Sakai set themselves up in business supplying simple, authentic and often very expensive tea utensils. Their influence over the development of the tea ceremony was therefore twofold: through the aesthetics of simplicity, as represented by Sen Rikyu, and through a strong trading monopoly on its vital commodities.

Yet this temptation to profit from the tea ceremony either in financial or political terms was foreign to Sen Rikyu's ideals. A visitor once asked Rikyu for the secret of the tea ceremony, and nothing better sums up the simplicity of its aesthetic experience better than the answer he gave, enshrined now as the *Seven Rules of Sen Rikyu*:

*Make a delicious bowl of tea; lay the charcoal so that it heats the water: arrange the flowers as they are in the field; in summer suggest coolness, in winter, warmth; do everything ahead of time; prepare for rain; and give those with whom you find yourself every consideration. There is no other secret.*

Like Sakai itself, Sen Rikyu represented an oasis of peace amidst the warlike world of the Sengoku Period, and it served him well. After Oda Nobunaga abolished the shogunate and occupied Kyoto in 1569 he turned his attentions to the independent 'free port' of Sakai, and his friendship with the local tea master Imai Sokyu, who also happened to be the owner of a munitions factory and an influential member of Sakai's governing body, greatly helped in securing the peaceful submission of the city. It was Imai Sokyu who introduced Sen Rikyu to Oda Nobunaga.

By that time Sen Rikyu had been performing the tea ceremony to great acclaim from at least the age of 15, and his meeting with the first of Japan's three unifiers not only enhanced his profile as a tea master but also added a whole new dimension to his life, because Nobunaga invited him to become his secretary and effectively his roving ambassador. No doubt the fact that a tea master enjoyed the most intimate private audiences with his hosts provided part of the reason for such an appointment, but Nobunaga, like so many of his contemporaries, was a genuine tea fanatic.

Sen Rikyu nonetheless performed his ambassadorial role with the same commitment and meticulous attention to fine detail that he gave to the tea ceremony, and there exists a letter which Rikyu sent to a merchant of Sakai, in which he forwards for his colleague's approval a draft letter from Nobunaga to Hideyoshi concerning the siege of Tottori. The fact that Sen Rikyu was entrusted with the details of a top-level military operation shows the esteem in which he was held.

When Nobunaga was murdered in 1582 and Hideyoshi took his place, Sen Rikyu was transferred to the service of Japan's new ruler. Toyotomi Hideyoshi was another devotee of the tea ceremony and became its greatest contemporary enthusiast. So impressed was he by Sen Rikyu's affinity for tea that Hideyoshi made him *tenka gosado* ('tea master of Japan') at a splendid tea ceremony held for the emperor at the imperial palace. No civilian of ignoble birth, far less the son of a fishmonger, had ever acquired such an honour in the entire history of Japan, and just as had been the case with Nobunaga, Hideyoshi continued to use Sen Rikyu's talents and connections at the highest political level. When Hideyoshi was off campaigning, Sen Rikyu stayed behind in Osaka castle and managed the place, with full access to his master's official correspondence. In one letter to a certain general he notes calmly: 'My custody of the castle is going well. Nothing has changed here.'

Evidence of Sen Rikyu's remarkable status is provided by his role in the negotiations that sought to avoid military action against

The interior of the tea house inside the grounds of Hirado castle, showing the simple yet beautiful interior decor.

the Shimazu family in 1586. Hideyoshi first addressed a threatening letter to the *daimyo* Shimazu Yoshihisa, in which he commanded him 'in the name of the emperor' to make peace with his Kyushu rivals and thereby avoid being attacked. When there was no reply from Yoshihisa, who regarded Hideyoshi as a jumped-up little peasant compared to his own aristocratic pedigree, Hideyoshi tried a different approach, and Sen Rikyu and Hosokawa Yusai wrote a joint letter to Ijuin Tadamune, a senior retainer of the Shimazu. This man was personally indebted to them both, because Sen Rikyu had taught him the tea ceremony and Hosokawa had taught him poetry. This second letter received a reply from Shimazu Yoshihisa himself, so in spite of all the social effects of the Sengoku Period, where the rule of the sword is popularly supposed never to have been questioned and was rarely disobeyed, the relationship between a disciple and his *sensei* (teacher) could be far more influential than a general's command.

In the event, the reply from Shimazu Yoshihisa was courteous but unyielding. He was determined to crush Otomo Sorin, his last remaining rival in Kyushu, and Hideyoshi's threat to assist Otomo with military force, even if delivered by a pair of living national treasures, was not going to intimidate him, so the next we hear of Sen Rikyu he is involved in the reception for Otomo Sorin, who arrived in Osaka to plead for Hideyoshi's aid in the early spring of 1586. Rikyu performed the tea ceremony after attending, in an official capacity, the meeting at which Otomo Sorin was formally received by Hideyoshi and his most intimate advisers. He then took Otomo Sorin on a tour of Osaka castle, and showed him Hideyoshi's golden tea room, which was the ultimate in unrestrained design. Nothing was discussed about military support at these meetings. That was left to a later meeting between Otomo and Hashiba Hidenaga, Hideyoshi's half-brother, and again Sen Rikyu played a vital role, as Otomo later recognised.

Several of Hideyoshi's generals were fortunate enough to be named among the 'Seven Disciples' of Sen Rikyu. One was

Gamo Ujisato, who had once been rebuked by the warlike and unusually anti-tea general Saito Toshikazu that 'a soldier should not allow anything to interfere with his profession'. Gamo saw some wisdom in this when Saito advised him in matters of siegework, but he never abandoned the tea ceremony, even when he became a *daimyo*.

Another example of Sen Rikyu's influence on the blend between warrior and tea master concerns Kamibayashi Masashige, called Chikuan, who served Tokugawa Ieyasu as samurai and tea master, and took two heads at the battle of Nagakute. Not wishing to lose his services through death in battle, Ieyasu compulsorily retired him, but when Fushimi castle was attacked in 1600, Chikuan turned up to help defend the place. The commander, Torii Mototada, tried to send him away, but Chikuan replied that he owed a debt to Ieyasu, and drew his sword to commit *hara kiri*, while threatening to 'go and make tea in hell'. Mototada stopped him from killing himself, and Chikuan entered

Tea utensils in a tea room in Nagasaki, showing the tea kettle and tea bowls.

the castle with a banner made from old bags for tea sewn together and a red headband round his forehead.

The most crucial relationship in Sen Rikyu's life was with Toyotomi Hideyoshi, who became his most influential patron and was most dependent upon his other services. A famous story told about Sen Rikyu and Hideyoshi concerns the tea master's garden, which was renowned for its beautiful morning glory flowers. Choosing the time when they would be in full bloom, Hideyoshi invited himself along, but when he arrived he found that all the plants had been stripped of their flowers. Believing that he had been deliberately insulted, Hideyoshi stormed into the tea house. He was stopped by the sight of one perfect morning glory flower, floating in a bowl of water.

Yet this famous story of anger being thwarted by aesthetics conceals the truth of the relationship between Hideyoshi and Sen Rikyu, which was gradually turning sour. That others were involved in Sen Rikyu falling out of favour is in little doubt, but after the Kyushu campaign times were changing, as was Hideyoshi's need for his skilled negotiator. Sen Rikyu had joined Hideyoshi's entourage when Hideyoshi still governed from the battlefield, and at this stage in his career the future dictator depended as much on negotiation as on military talent. Those of his generals who happened to possess diplomatic and political skills were frequently needed on the battlefield, so Sen Rikyu filled a very important niche, and his unquestioned authority on the tea ceremony meant that he controlled the means of negotiation as much as its content.

However, others sought promotion for themselves to the ranks of Hideyoshi's closest advisers, and as Hideyoshi's rule over Japan grew closer to its final totality, even tea enthusiasts saw no place in their councils for Sen Rikyu. When in 1591 Sen Rikyu was reprimanded for mishandling the discussions over the submission of Date Masamune from northern Japan, it was obvious to all that a rift had developed between Hideyoshi and his closest confidant. A few weeks later Sen Rikyu received orders to leave Kyoto for Sakai. He was escorted to the boat like a prisoner, under cover of darkness, and so secret was his going that only two *daimyo* from among his many disciples came to see him off. They were similarly mystified when Rikyu was recalled shortly afterwards and ordered to commit *hara kiri* in an enclosed building, heavily guarded by 3,000 men.

Rumours and conspiracy theories about Sen Rikyu's forced suicide began immediately and have continued to this day. Ideas range from his refusal to allow his daughter to become Hideyoshi's concubine, to his involvement in a plot to have Hideyoshi poisoned – a form of assassination, of course, for which tea masters were ideally placed. It also showed how vulnerable a tea master,

even the greatest tea master of all, was compared to a disgraced *daimyo*, who sometimes had the opportunity to wipe out his disgrace on the battlefield. The son of a fish merchant could be made to fall as rapidly as he had once risen. The *Tamon-In nikki* gives an account of his death as follows, but its speculation about the motive is not necessarily any more accurate that any other theory.

*Possibly on the grounds that in recent years he had prepared new fashioned utensils and sold them at high prices – the height of venality – the Kampaku's (Hideyoshi's) anger was suddenly kindled and he immediately ordered that he be crucified. As he apologised profusely, a statue that had been made and placed at Shibano was crucified instead.*

The reference to the statue concerns a wooden effigy of Sen Rikyu that was placed in the Daitokuji in Kyoto. This had certainly enraged Hideyoshi, and to the chronicler the fact that Sen Rikyu was allowed to commit *hara kiri* like a noble samurai, rather than be crucified like a common criminal, showed Hideyoshi's generosity. It may also have shown real regret, because even after his death Sen Rikyu was on Hideyoshi's mind, although whether with expressions of guilt or genuine feelings of loss is hard to fathom. When Hideyoshi wrote a letter commissioning the building of Fushimi castle, as well as 'making it hard to attack from the giant catfish' (i.e. earthquake proof) he insists that the castle's construction should be done 'in accordance with Rikyu's preference and discretion', and this was one year after the forced suicide.

Sen Rikyu is remembered in Japan today as the man who made the tea ceremony what it is, and in so doing influenced an entire generation of Japanese generals and politicians, in a unique contribution to samurai life and history that was both civil and civilised. No samurai general could have expected so warm and long-lasting an epitaph.

# The triumph of the Tokugawa

Following the successful outcome of the siege of Odawara in 1590, Tokugawa Ieyasu was granted the Hojo territories in fief, and moved his capital to Edo. The distance of his domains from Kyushu allowed him to avoid service during the invasion of Korea – a futile and bloody war that sapped the strength of many of his contemporaries. The invasion had ended when Hideyoshi died in the manner that all dictators dread, leaving his infant son Toyotomi Hideyori to inherit newly unified Japan. The *daimyo* who had survived or avoided the decimation of the Korean War then divided into two armed camps and fought each other at the famous battle of Sekigahara in 1600. On one side was a coalition under the command of Ishida Mitsunari, who supported the cause of the infant Hideyori. They were called the

Tokugawa Ieyasu as depicted in the effigy of him situated in the Tokugawa family temple of Daijuji in Okazaki.

Western Army. Opposing them was Tokugawa Ieyasu, who believed that only he had the resources to manage the newly unified empire. His supporters were called the Eastern Army, and they marched towards Osaka from Edo.

Great danger was caused for Ieyasu when his son Hidetada was delayed at Ueda, one of several sieges that took place as the two sides tried to capture each other's castles, but the final outcome of the contest was decided not by a siege but by an epic field encounter in a narrow valley through which ran the Nakasendo road. The battle of Sekigahara proved to be one of the most decisive battles in Japanese history. Ishida Mitsunari advanced his army to block Ieyasu's advance towards Kyoto and Osaka, and the issue was settled with much bloodshed.

When the fighting commenced that foggy October morning, Ieyasu's vanguard advanced under Fukushima Masanori and Ii Naomasa.

Honda Tadakatsu, the companion of Tokugawa Ieyasu in all his battles, is shown here in action at the famous battle of Sekigahara.

The latter led his 'Red Devils', so-called because of their red-lacquered armour, who first moved against the troops of Ukita Hideie, and then switched their attack to the Shimazu of Satsuma. The outcome of the battle was very much in the balance until Kobayakawa Hideaki (one of Ishida Mitsunari's best generals) dramatically changed sides in favour of the Tokugawa and attacked the western contingent nearest to his position. This was

the turning point in the struggle. Ishida
Mitsunari tried to hold firm, but the Shimazu
pulled back and, as the Western Army began
to withdraw, the Shimazu began a gallant
rearguard action. The pursuing Ii bore the
main brunt of their brave and stubborn
endeavour. When contingents of the Western
Army were seen withdrawing, Tokugawa
Ieyasu ordered a general advance. Up to that

Single combat with sword and spear during the decisive
battle of Sekigahara.

point he had not worn his helmet, but with
the words 'After a victory tighten your helmet
cords,' he completed his arming and followed
his troops to victory. Ishida Mitsunari was
captured alive, and his castle at Sawayama was
burned to the ground.

## The Osaka campaigns

In the immediate aftermath of Sekigahara there was little opposition left to prevent Tokugawa Ieyasu taking the title of shogun, which he alone among the three unifiers was able to do because of his distant descent from the Minamoto family. He was formally proclaimed shogun in 1603, and set in motion a number of schemes to consolidate his family's position. These included a massive redistribution of fiefs, with the traditional allies of the Tokugawa and their hereditary retainers (the fudai) being given key territories where they could control dangerous neighbours. Those who had opposed Ieyasu at Sekigahara by word or deed (the tozama) found themselves moved to the far corners of Japan. Needless to say, this provoked great resentment among the losers, and the greatest loser of all was Hideyori, the heir of Toyotomi Hideyoshi, who had effectively been disinherited by Ieyasu's victory at Sekigahara and his subsequent acquisition of the title of shogun.

There were many others who resented the Tokugawa rise to power, including thousands of samurai whose lords had been killed at Sekigahara or who had had their lands confiscated. They were now *ronin* ('men of the waves' or unemployed samurai) and in 1614 they flocked to join Hideyori's standard when he began to pack into his late father's mighty edifice of Osaka castle every element of military opposition to the Tokugawa takeover. This was a severe challenge to the Tokugawa hegemony, and there was no alternative but to mount a siege against Osaka, where the outer walls measured 12 miles in circumference.

One of the first actions at Osaka took place during the so-called Winter Campaign of 1614/15. The Ii family's Red Devils attacked the huge complex of earthworks built to the south of the castle and known from the name of its commander as the Sanada-maru, or Sanada Barbican. The Ii were badly mauled during the fighting but would not withdraw. It is by no means clear whether this was from sheer samurai

stubbornness and determination to complete the job or a simple lack of communication from headquarters in all the noise and the smoke, but those to their rear knew that the Ii had to pull back or they would be annihilated. A commander called Miura (identified as a ninja) solved the problem very neatly by ordering his men to fire against the backs of the Red Devils. This had the result of forcing the Ii to 'attack to safety' when they reacted as expected, and the Red Devils survived to fight another day.

That day was not long in coming, and the Summer Campaign of Osaka in 1615 was to be the last time the Red Devils would go into battle. Their most celebrated episode was the battle of Wakae. This was one of a number of engagements that took place some distance from Osaka castle itself prior to the main assault on the fortress. The villages of Wakae and Yao, which are now suburbs of Greater Osaka, were then tiny hamlets in the middle of rice fields. Yao was the first encounter where the Todo family on the Tokugawa side came off very badly, but out on their left flank the Red Devils soon came to grips with one of the most senior commanders on the Osaka side – Kimura Shigenari. When the Todo were defeated the Ii were hurriedly ordered into position near Wakae. Beginning with a volley from their arquebusiers, the Ii under Naotaka charged forward with allied units on their flanks. Having fired their arquebuses, the ashigaru gunners shouldered their weapons and ran along beside the bulk of the cavalry and the large number of foot soldiers carrying the red banners.

The Kimura samurai were soon in full retreat. Kimura Shigenari was killed and his head was cut off, and several of the Ii samurai claimed the credit for this illustrious prize. When the head was taken to Tokugawa Ieyasu, who shared the command at Osaka with the current shogun Hidetada, he noted that Kimura Shigenari had burned incense inside his helmet prior to the battle so as to make his severed head a more attractive trophy. Ieyasu commended the practice to his followers.

Throughout the long siege of Osaka a new element in Japanese warfare made its presence noisily felt. For the first time in samurai history a fortress was subjected to an artillery bombardment on a European scale. The cannon were all obtained from visiting European ships, and so skilled did the Japanese gunners become that they succeeded in placing a cannonball into Hideyori's private apartments from a considerable distance. Prior to the siege, Tokugawa Ieyasu also bought up all the gunpowder he could lay his hands on. Culverins and sakers are the two types of cannon mentioned at Osaka, and the former could deliver a cannonball over the distance of a mile. By contrast, the Toyotomi side only had comparatively weak breech loaders and catapults.

The siege of Osaka finished with the huge battle of Tennoji in the summer of 1615, fought on the fields to the south of the fortress. The move was initiated by Toyotomi Hideyori, who planned to march out of the castle under his late father's 'thousand gourd standard' when the Tokugawa were on the point of being defeated. Unfortunately things did not go according to plan, and Sanada Yukimura, the best general on the Osaka side, was killed fighting. Ii Naotaka's Red Devils played a major role in the battle alongside the survivors of the Todo against the survivors of the Kimura. A worrying moment occurred when a delayed-action landmine, a clever Chinese device, exploded under the Todo troops.

When the Tokugawa army rallied and Osaka castle looked about to fall, Tokugawa Ieyasu entrusted Ii Naotaka with the task of keeping watch over Toyotomi Hideyori and his family and of securing the castle itself. Ii

The restored keep of Osaka castle, site of the great siege of 1614/15 where the Toyotomi family were finally destroyed.

Kimura Shigenari, one of the defenders of Osaka castle, depicted on this modern painting at the shrine to him on the site of the battle of Wakae, where he was killed.

Naotaka interpreted these orders somewhat generously as an invitation to open up on the castle with every piece of artillery he possessed, and soon the keep was in flames. Toyotomi Hideyori committed suicide, and all his family were executed to stamp out the Toyotomi line forever. With the fall of Osaka castle the opposition to the Tokugawa was over, and the Sengoku Period came to an end.

# Japan closes its doors

To some extent the consequences of the wars of the Sengoku Period may be felt in Japan to this day, not as a direct result of the fighting that took place so long ago, but more because of the isolationist measures the Tokugawa shoguns then put in place to prevent any more wars happening. One major element in their polity was the *baku han* system, whereby national government was provided by the *bakufu* or shogunate, and local government by the *daimyo*'s fiefs or *han*.

Like everything else in Tokugawa Japan, there were regulations governing the smallest detail of everyday life. The *daimyo*'s castle became the focal point for local administration, and many were rebuilt or extended. Yet along with the rebuilding and redevelopment of provincial castles, many were destroyed under the policy of 'one province, one castle'. The result was that the mighty fortresses we see today became the centre of a *daimyo*'s territory in a more decisive and defined way than ever before. Some, like Himeji, Matsumoto and Hikone, are perfectly preserved. Trade flourished in the castle towns, and many merchants grew richer than the samurai, who were supposed to have no trade beyond that of serving as a loyal warrior.

The additional policy of settling potential rebels in distant fiefs with loyal *daimyo* to watch over them was enhanced by a development of the Japanese tradition of taking hostages to ensure good behaviour. So while all the *daimyo* lived in their castle towns from where they governed their provinces, their wives and children were required to live in Edo, right under the eyes of the shogun. The wisdom of this move was seen in 1638 when the Shimabara Rebellion broke out. It started as a peasant revolt and drew in dispossessed samurai; none of the *daimyo* broke ranks to join them. The final refinement of the system was to require the *daimyo* to make regular visits to Edo to pay their respects to the shogun. This had the result of forcing all the armies of Japan to spend most of their time and resources marching from one end of the archipelago to the other.

The next measure was a complete reversal of the policy of encouraging foreign trade and exploration that had characterised the first decade of the 17th century and led to such adventurers as Yamada Nagamasa sailing to Formosa (Taiwan) and Siam (Thailand). Instead Tokugawa Japan increasingly turned in on itself. Fear of European influence led first to a ban on Christianity and then to a ban on foreign trade. Only China and Korea were exempt, and their trade contacts were strictly controlled. Apart from a tiny trading post called Dejima in Nagasaki harbour, where the Protestant Dutch (who could be relied upon not to spread the Jesuits' messages) were allowed very limited access, Japan closed its doors to the outside world.

All these measures came about because the Tokugawa shoguns feared a return to the dark days of the Sengoku Period. Two centuries of peace followed, out of which emerged modern Japan and a world very different from the one that had once known a century and a half of war.

# Technical details

## Written messages in battle

Written messages were a vital means of strategic communication during the Sengoku Period, and a particularly striking example was used at the castle of Kangui in Korea in 1593. Kuroda Nagamasa had dispatched a messenger to the castle to enquire how they were standing up to the Chinese advance, so the garrison wrote a letter back which read: 'Urgent warning, the enemy army have crossed the river in the middle of the night and are establishing lines on this side, so that we will soon be crossing swords in battle. Please send out troops quickly.' But the hero Awayama Shiro'emon realised that there was no time to get reinforcements to them, and with the words: 'This is in fact a suicide note!', he crossed out 'Please send out troops quickly' and rewriting it as 'Please rest easily' led the garrison in a spirited attack.

The strangest political device set in place by the Tokugawa was to require the *daimyo* and their armies to make regular visits to Edo at often enormous expense. One such procession is shown in this scroll.

## Trumpet calls

The *Gunji Yoshu* lists the conch shell trumpet calls used in a samurai army. This provided an important means of audible communication and the patterns used in some of them have a religious significance.

First, there was a sequence of three conch signals for making ready for departure. On the first call eating must be abandoned or not begun. On the second the soldier must get himself ready, and on the third depart, with the vanguard taking the lead and the other units following. The call was a set of nine conch blows, performed successively three times, nine times and 27 times. On actual departure the call was one single blow, then five sets of five blows, three sets of three blows, seven sets of seven blows, five sets of five blows, three sets of three blows and one single final blow, a pattern which apparently follows the rhythm of a particular Buddhist chant in Sanskrit.

The conch was also used for time-keeping. During the night in an army's encampment the call was two sets of four conch blows.

This was given three times during the night: at the beginning of the Hour of the Rat (11.00pm to 1.00am), the Hour of the Ox (1.00am to 3.00am) and the hour of the Tiger (3.00am to 5.00am). There was, in addition, a midday call which was a simple sequence of five, three, then seven conch blows. The call for the initial preparation of an army was three sets of five conch blows, the number five signifying the five sacred colours. For bringing the soldiers together, the call was five sets of five conch blows, the number 25 standing for the number of bodhisattvas (as this was how many there were supposed to be in the Buddhist heaven).

For advancing one's army by night, the call was seven conch blows, to which the reply of 10 conch blows was given in confirmation. In order to make it known to one's allies that a night attack was taking place, the call was eight sets of eight conch blows, the number eight representing Hachiman, the god of war, whose name literally reads 'eight banners'. The call to be given when it became apparent that the enemy was showing signs of being defeated was four sets of four conch blows, then four blows, then two sets of six blows, then four blows. On this occasion the conch blowing also set the pace of the advance along with the drums. If it appeared that one's allies were not aware of this situation, it was communicated to them by three sets of three conch blows. To summon allies to one's aid, the sequence was five, seven, five and three conch blows.

The conch call to order the extermination of an enemy was seven sets of seven conch blows, then five sets of five conch blows and three sets of three conch blows. These should finish with long blasts. The conch call for striking camp was a sequence of five sets of five conch blows, followed by seven sets of seven and three sets of three conch blows. The conch call for scouts approaching was three sets of three conch blows given by the sentries keeping watch in a castle or a camp. In all the above, the *Gunji Yoshu* states that when the conch is blown, the notes should not be stopped or cut short, and that a note

should begin quietly and be raised in pitch to end with a high note.

## The Christian *daimyo*

Among the religious beliefs expressed by the samurai of the Sengoku Period, there was a small but influential minority who professed Christianity. One of the army divisions that invaded Korea was almost entirely composed of Christian samurai, whose faith arose from the missionary work of Jesuits from 1549. The Jesuits were most active, and most successful, in Kyushu, where there were several Christian *daimyo* by the 1590s. The extent to which their belief was no more than a bargaining counter for obtaining favours from European merchants is still a matter of controversy, but it is undoubtedly true that thousands of their followers, including peasants and fisherfolk, were fervent Christians and suffered persecution as a result.

The most prominent *daimyo* to benefit from European influence was Oda Nobunaga, who never converted. Instead he allowed the missionaries to operate freely in his territories, seeing them as a counter to the militant Buddhists who were his greatest enemies.

The persecution of Christians dates from 1597, when Hideyoshi became alarmed by the influence of European powers who might be able to use Christianity as a Trojan horse. In Nagasaki 26 martyrs were crucified that year, but it was only when the Tokugawa regime tried to close Japan off from European influence that Christianity disappeared from Japanese society. Yet even then the faith survived underground as the Kakure or 'Hidden Christians', and the famous Shimabara Rebellion of 1637/38 was a Christian peasants' revolt led by the messianic figure of Amakusa Shiro.

## Ninja

The topic of ninja remains one of the most fascinating mysteries of Japanese warfare in

the Sengoku Period. The ninja were the secret agents and assassins who supposedly belonged to covert brotherhoods. The word crops up again and again in the chronicles, usually in the context of secret intelligence gathering. Many opportune deaths may possibly be credited to ninja activities, but as they were so secret it is impossible to prove any veracity.

The traditional ninja garb of a full black costume is every bit as tantalising. There are no authentic written accounts of ninja dressed in black. Usually they appear to have disguised themselves to blend in with the garrison of a castle, for example. The earliest pictorial reference is a book illustration of 1801, which shows a ninja climbing into a

LEFT Amakusa Shiro, the leader of the unsuccessful Christian Shimabara Rebellion of 1638, which was crushed by the Tokugawa army.

BELOW The blowing of a *horagai* (shell trumpet) by a yamabushi. The *horagai* was one of the most useful audible communication devices.

castle wearing what everyone would immediately recognise as a ninja costume. However, it could simply be that it is pictures like these that have given us our image of the ninja rather than vice versa, and it is a long-standing convention in Japan, seen today in the Bunraku puppet theatre, that to dress a character in black is to indicate to the viewer that he cannot see that person. To depict a silent assassin in an identical way would therefore be perfectly natural, and need not imply that the resulting illustration was in any way a 'portrait of a ninja'.

The other image of the ninja as a superhuman who can fly and do magic, also has a surprisingly long history in Japan, but many of the tales have become mixed up with other legends. Nevertheless, the ways of the ninja are an unavoidable part of Sengoku warfare, even though their secretive and underhand methods contrasted sharply with the ideal of the noble samurai facing squarely on to his enemy.

## Samurai cavalry tactics

In contemporary writings three ways of carrying out a cavalry attack were identified:

*Norikomi*
In a situation where the enemy have advanced close to one's own lines, a small number of horsemen are sent out as scouts. They ride into the enemy lines, cause a disturbance and withdraw as a 'reconnaissance in force'.

*Norikiri*
In the middle of a battle when the enemy lines have been broken, a section of five to 10 horsemen ride in suddenly to attack an enemy who have wavered, throwing them into confusion.

*Norikuzushi*
The horsemen and infantry on foot charge into the ranks of missile troops, breaking them in one go and overrunning them.

This third technique was regarded as the particular strong point of the mighty Takeda clan, who dominated central Japan from the 1530s under the *daimyo* Takeda Shingen, one of the greatest commanders of the Sengoku Period. 'The strength of the Takeda was in their cavalry' is a truism of Japanese history, and Takeda Shingen has sometimes been compared to Napoleon in his use of mounted troops, or even regarded as using horsemen like a squadron of tanks. At the height of its powers the Takeda army consisted of 30,000 men of whom 3,000 were horsemen. The number actually mobilised on a battlefield may have differed from time to time, but the proportion of horsemen to foot would be about the same.

The Takeda acquired a fearsome reputation for this type of warfare. Eastern Japan was always famed for horses, and in the *Shinchokoki* it says: 'The Kanto-shu are skilled on horses.' From the Nara Period onwards came the swift horses called 'the black horses of Kai', and this reputation continued into the Sengoku Period, when the Takeda ruled that province. The Takeda horses were not frightened by the sound of guns or the smell of burning, and there was an abundant supply of mounts. The Takeda samurai were also very good horsemen. From birth the Kai warrior was intimate with horses, and trust developed between horse and rider.

# Further reading

The main sources for this book are in the Japanese language, of which the series *Rekishi Gunzo* is the most accessible. Many of its superbly illustrated volumes cover the Sengoku Period.

In English the most reliable general background reading may be found in *The Cambridge History of Japan* and G.B. Sansom's three volume *History of Japan*. For those readers wishing to read more about the two individuals highlighted here the 'Precepts' of Kato Kiyomasa may be read in full in W.S. Watson's *Ideals of the Samurai* (Ohara 1982). An excelent article entitled 'Tea and Counsel: The Political Role of Sen Rikyu' by B.M.

Bodart is reprinted in *The Samurai Tradition* (Japan Library 2000) a compilation of academic articles to which I provide an introduction.

Of my own works *Samurai Warfare* (Cassels 1996) and *The Samurai Sourcebook* (Cassels 1998) provide a wealth of technical detail to complement this book. For detailed study of battles of the period see my two Osprey Campaigns volumes *Nagashino 1575* (2000) and *Kawanakajima 1553-64* (publication forthcoming) and A. Bryant's *Sekigahara 1600* (1995). The Korean campaign is covered in my *Samurai Invasion: Japan's Korean War 1592-98* (Cassells 2002).

# Index